"This Coast Doesn't Fit Me Anymore"

Sheila J. Spencer

Sheila J. Spencer
THIS COAT DOESN'T FIT ME ANYMORE: Coats weren't made to last forever
Copyright© November 8, 2004

Requests for information should be addressed to:
S.O.L.A.C.E. International Publishing Co.
P.O. Box 680673
Orlando, Florida 32868
(800) 877-2577
www.sheilajministries.com

All rights reserved. No part of this book may be reproduced, stored in a retrieval system or transmitted in any form or by any means - electronic, mechanical, photocopy, recording, or otherwise - without prior written permission of the copyright owner, except by a reviewer who wishes to quote brief passages in connection with a review for inclusion in a magazine, newspaper, or broadcast.

All scripture quotations are taken from The Holy Bible, King James Version.

ISBN: 0-9768452-0-2

Printed in the United States of America.

Foreword

"Losing a spouse is never easy, and addressing the results affects the present and a myriad of issues and emotions that require special attention. Sheila Spencer delicately addresses those issues with empathy while offering sound advice and good counsel to widows and widowers."

Dr. Paula White -
Without Walls International Church

Endorsed by
Dr. Gloria Williams

In the book "This Coat Doesn't Fit Me Anymore," Prophetess Sheila J. Spencer takes us stage by stage into what can be the growth patterns for our individual Christian life styles. The overwhelming theme in this book is that times change, seasons change, situations and circumstances change, we change and life itself changes. However, in the midst of all the change what is constant is God. God never changes and he gives us the power and authority to succeed in life throughout all of the "Coat" changes. As we read this book we will measure the Coat we have on right now!

Dr. Gloria Y. Williams -
Jesus People Ministries of Miami

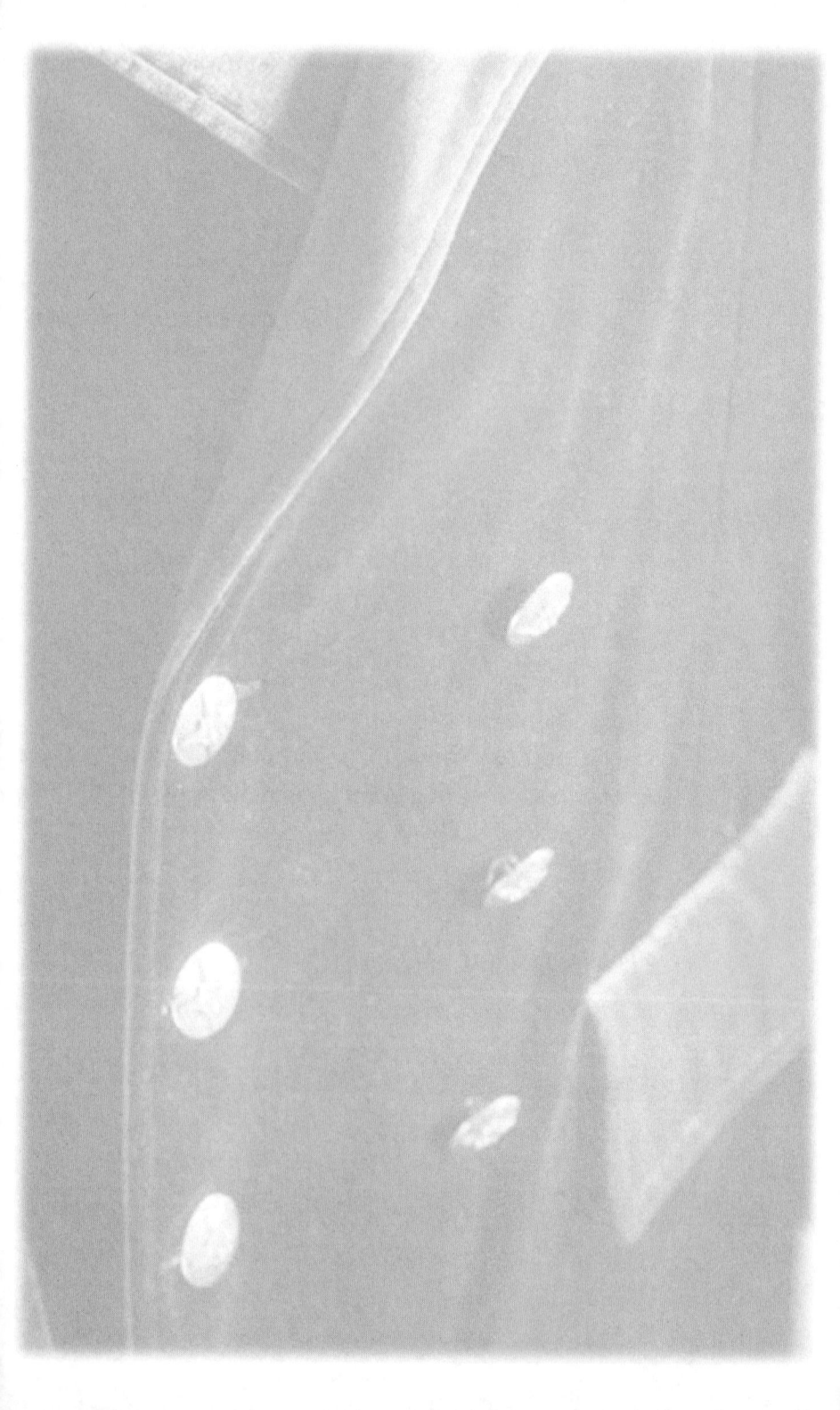

Endorsements

In the book "This Coat Doesn't Fit Me Anymore," Prophetess Sheila J. Spencer takes us stage by stage into what can be the growth patterns for our individual Christian life styles. The overwhelming theme in this book is that times change, seasons change, situations and circumstances change, we change and life itself changes. However, in the midst of all the change what is constant is God. God never changes and he gives us the power and authority to succeed in life throughout all of the "Coat" changes. As we read this book we will measure the Coat we have on right now!
Bishop Isaiah and Dr. Gloria Y. Williams - Jesus People Ministries of Miami

This dynamic book will give you revelatory insight into the spiritual journey of how God transitions your life for new levels of increase. "This Coat Doesn't Fit Me Anymore" gives you strategic keys that will build your faith so that you may walk through difficult circumstances with the peace of God in your heart. Prophetess Sheila Spencer opens her heart and becomes intimate with the reader to deal with how to move forward when a spouse dies. Prophetess Sheila Spencer's first hand experiences and examples distinguishes this book from the rest. "This Coat Doesn't Fit Me Anymore" gives strength and hope to those that desperately feel hope is gone.
Dr. Zachary and Pastor Riva Timms - New Destiny Christian Center, Inc.

"Don't abort your destiny in God by reluctance to shed an old coat that no longer suits you. This book will help you, with scripture example after example, to disown what you've outgrown and get the perfect fit in Him, for God will not usher you into a new season without giving you a new coat. Don't put this book on the shelf untouched. You'll miss a blessing."
Bishop Harold and Pastor Brenda Ray - Redemptive Life Fellowship

"This Coat Doesn't Fit Me Anymore" is a powerful, penetrating, prophetic book that speaks of the travails of Pastor/Prophetess Sheila J. Spencer. She profoundly expounds upon the transitional stages of dealing with the loss of a spouse while yet responsible for a functioning full time ministry. This book is cutting edge, impact full, and certainly useful to anyone desiring to operate ministry at a supernatural level.

Pastors Randall & Sharlene Holts - New Hope MBC of Miami, Inc.

Prophetess Spencer has received a revelation from the Lord that will no doubt help many enter into their season of grace. This book I believe will inspire its reader to recognize that the anointing on their lives is liken to that of a coat. These coats may change from time to time, and it will sometimes result in suffering and discomfort. Prophetess Spencer however, illustrates so clearly that during this process God will have to endure it, and reap the benefits from others.

Pastor Horace L Mingo - Jesus People of Gainesville

I highly recommend this book for all that have a strong calling upon their life. WOW - As I read through the pages of this book I found myself shaking my head and saying Amen out loud. This book reveals and defines the coats that Christ wore, and how He never kept them on long than needed, as he walked in what His Father had tailor made for Him. Written wisely and purposefully all can learn and understand how Christ demonstrated the power of forgiveness.

Pastor Philip and Debbie Meeks - Associated Pastor, Time of Refreshing

I love it when great Bible stories and great truths are presented with strong visible pictures. Prophetess Spencer has done this so effectively through using something that we are all acquainted to bring revelation truth from the Word of God. This is exciting because presented this way the great truths in this book will never be forgotten and will continue to impact the reader throughout their life and ministry.
God bless and I pray much success with your book.

Dr. C. Faith Fredrick, - CEO/President, Faith Christian University.

The Prophetess once again brings forth great revelation in this book. Our spiritual eyes were "slammed" wide open, our natural eyes wept and our hearts were filled with encouragement. Once again, this great woman of God impacted our lives. We pray God gives you the insight He has given us through this book.

Ed and Debbie Campany - Campany, Enterprise

My wife and I share a relationship with Pastor Spencer and are quit aware of her past struggles. Analogies are used in this book that are understandable today to those that are no scholar no less to those who are not bible scholars. Pastor Spencer goes through the explanation of Hannah, Joseph, Samuel and most of all Jesus Christ. This book explains in detail how these characters fit in the design that God has for them and explains to us the design that God has for us.

If you have never had any adversities in your life that cost you much, you are a candidate to be blessed. Sheila J. Spencer very own pain, suffering, healing and deliverance should give hope to those who could not see hope. We encourage you to get this book allow Pastor Spencer to size the coat as well as when you should change into a new one. We promise you, this book is most beneficial.

Pastor William and Mary Blue -
Directors Pastoral Alliance, Bishop T.D. Jakes
Potters House International Church

Contents

	Acknowledgments	1
	Introduction	2
One	Samuel's Coat	5
Two	Joseph's Coat	17
Three	Your Coat Doesn't Fit Me	25
Four	The Political Coat	33
Five	The Prophetic Coat	43
Six	The Widow's Coat	63
Seven	The Widow's Road To Recovery	79
Eight	The Final Tally	89

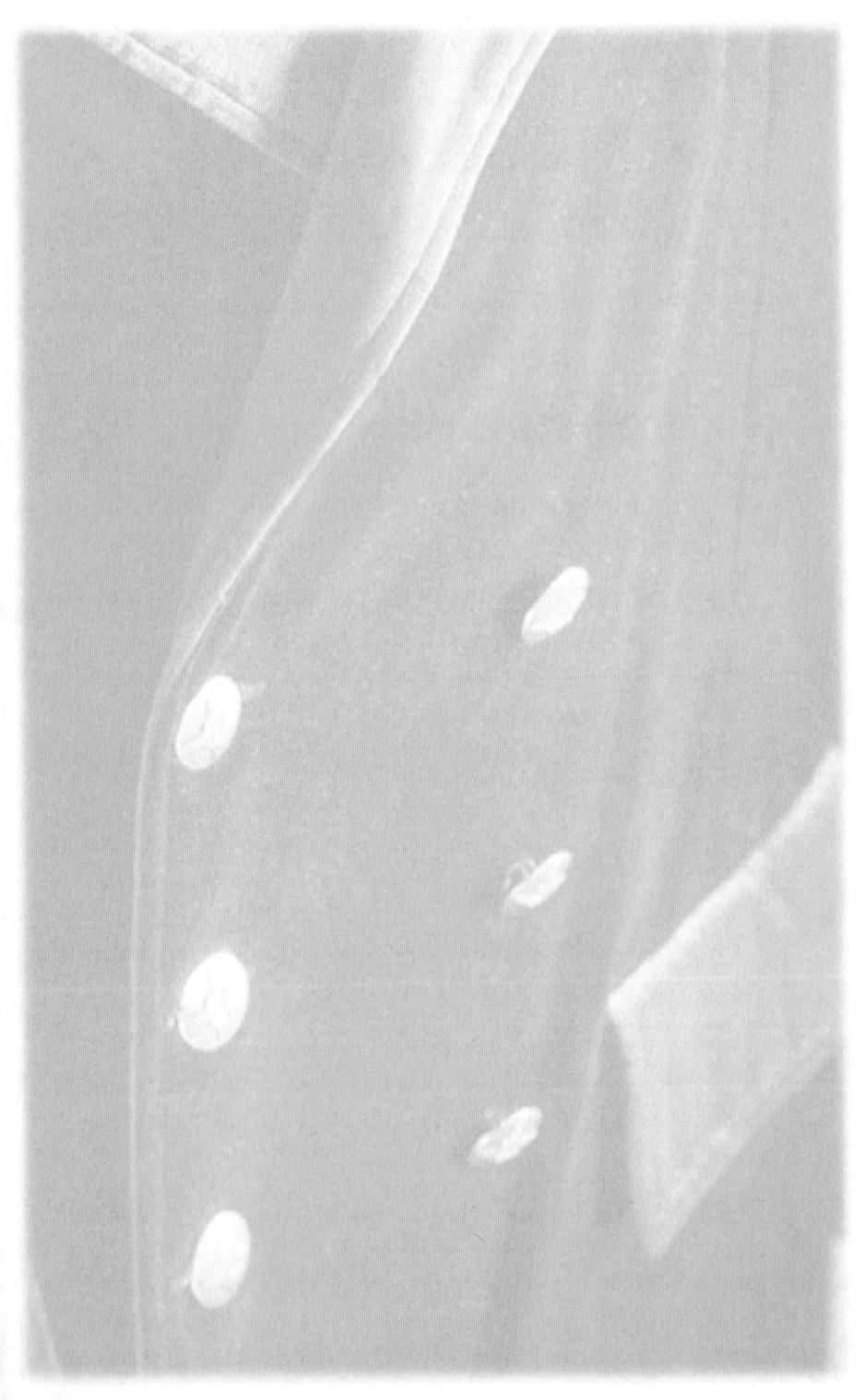

Acknowledgments

There are a lot people who have encouraged me throughout this writing process. It is great to have people in your life that can see what you cannot see. They allow the Holy Spirit to use them in an awesome way and they take the time to invest in you. Their love, strength and support cause you to endure and to go after your dreams. I am thankful for the people God has placed in my life.

I am grateful first and foremost to have children who feel so strongly that they believe that whatever I set my mind to do that indeed I can do it. To my daughter Temeka, I am exceptionally blessed to have a daughter who possesses extraordinary gifts. Your creative skills have produced a quality book.

To Kelly who supports me in all I do, your passion is visible. To my only son Jesse who feels there is no other mother in the world like me. Thanks to my grandson Junior, you are quite photogenic. Your face makes the cover – adorable. Thanks to my grandchildren, Austin, Aaliahya, Shyla and Dallas.

To the Honorable Bishop T.D. Jakes and Lady Serita Jakes, you have paved the way of success. Thank you for teaching me how to Maximize the Moment. You have indeed influenced my life through your prolific teaching and dedication to the Gospel. Thank you for all you have done for the Body of Christ.

Thank you Dawn for your passion. I had the vision to write this book. I appreciate your support and the long hours you put into this project. I also thank you for your creativity that helped me develop this book. I will be forever grateful.

To Pastor Deborah and Philip Meeks, your friendship has been extraordinary and ordained of God. To Pastor Zachery and Riva Tims, who leaped to the occasion to help, assist and guide me. This book would not have been birthed if it had not been for your support. Special thank you to my partners Ed and Debbie Campany. Your support is undeniable.

Thank you Cindy for your vision and your extraordinary skills and insights; you produced an outstanding cover & book layout. Your hard work and labor is indeed appreciated. To Jerry, thank you for your gifted abilities and the passion that you share in this project. To my Editor, Reva, whose prolific literary experiences and creativity took my vision and developed a great book. Thank you for your labor and hard work. Thank you to the entire First Printing and Copy Center staff.

Thank you Sonya and Revenia for your love and support.

Thank you Bishop Robert Joyce for your support. You are indeed an inspiration.

Special thanks to Pastor William and Lady Blue for your support.

To entire staff CDO Mr. Oliver, special thanks to James Ford, Wilhemina for your support. To my publishing and printing company SOLACE staff: Temeka, Kelly, Dawn, Sonya, and Revenia.

Introduction

I was inspired to write this book first and foremost by the Holy Spirit, along with my everyday journeys. This book draws important lessons from the lives of great men and women of God, along with events in my life.

There are several chapters within my first book entitled: "This Coat Doesn't Fit Me Anymore." These chapters glimpse into the lives of godly men and women with delegated coat changes. Coats are a metaphor for the situations that we go through in the different phases of our lives. God predestines the coat that is chosen for you. When you choose to put on a coat that is picked out by someone else, your destiny is delayed and your journey that was made straight now becomes a winding road.

This book peers into the depths of animosity, betrayal, and giving up what you have desperately awaited. We are sometimes held captive by our struggles and failures. But this coat book declares that you must seize the advantage of God's extended mercy and with each trial gain new lengths and depths in your spiritual walk.

I believe this book is designed to release men and women alike who have been trapped in the same stage of life for too long. They continue to wear coats that are too small for them because they fear the unknown. These fears can send you into a frustrating cycle as you find yourself circling the same mountain year after year.

Many people sense that there is a change heading our way. It is a wave of hope waiting inside the human spirit. That wave of hope tells us that help is on the way, in spite of the conditions of our nation, our churches and communities. This book wants to fuel the fire even more. It is also written for the average person so that you may understand that through the phases of life, coat changes will come and you must embrace them in order to advance in the kingdom of God.

So prepare yourself to put on the proper coat for whatever season you may be in, because wearing the wrong coat in the wrong season will bring about discomfort. As you read this book, take inventory on the choosing of your coats, and by the end of this book, you will find yourself a hero by pursuing, adapting, and conquering.

People are not born heroes, but become heroes by conquering their daily challenges without reprimanding their victories.

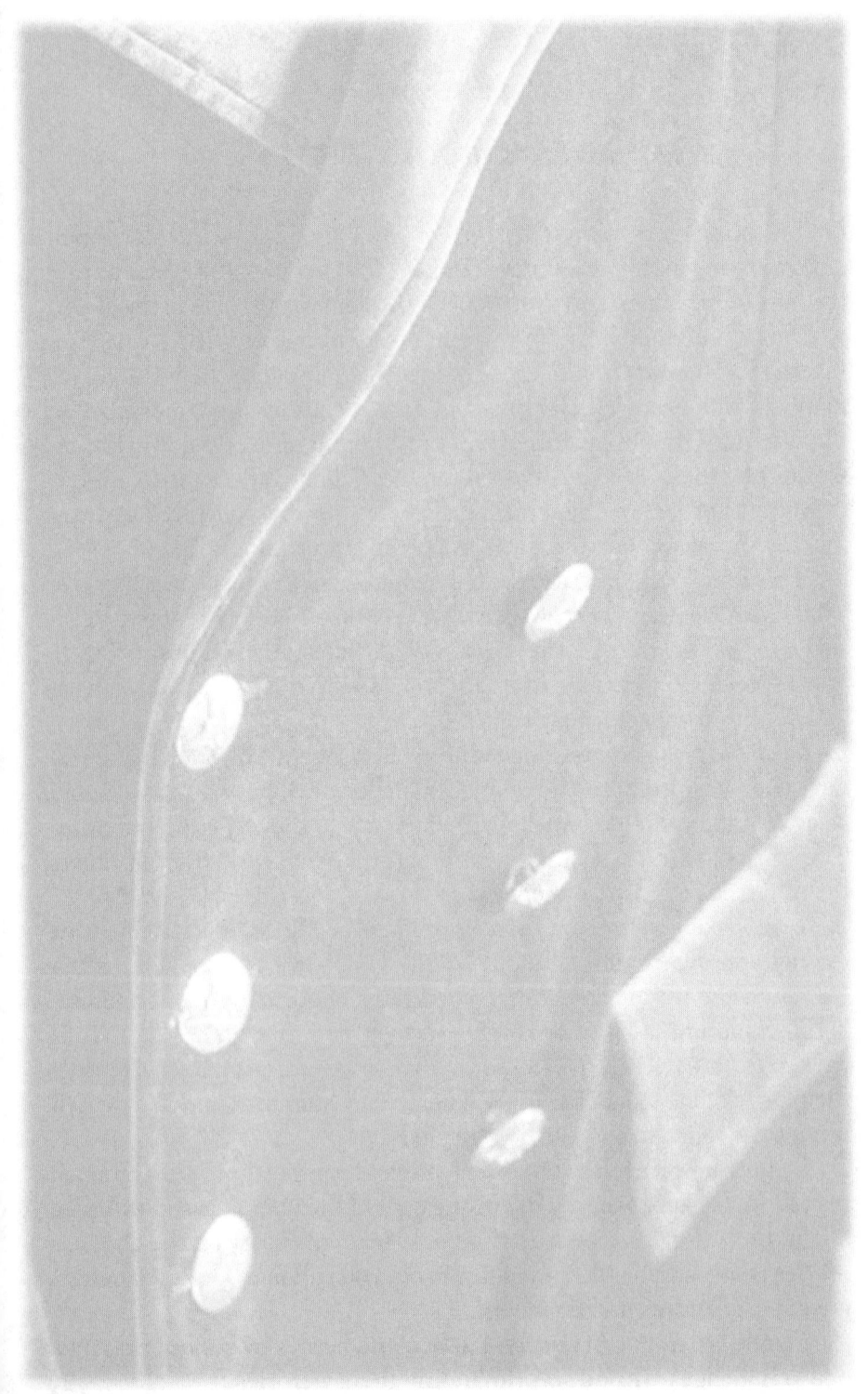

Chapter 1

Samuel's Coat
Samuel the Little Boy
1 Samuel 2:17-19

Coats are a metaphor for the situations that we go through in the different phases of our lives. The coat that is chosen for you is the predestination of God. When you choose to put on a coat that is picked out by someone else, your destiny is delayed and your journey that was made straight now becomes a winding road.

This book permits you to peer into the depths of animosity, betrayal, and giving up what you have desperately awaited. We are sometimes held captive by our struggles and failures. But this coat book shows you that you must seize the advantage of God's extended mercy and with each trial, you gain new depths in your spiritual walk.

So prepare yourself to put on the proper coat for whatever season you may be in, because wearing the wrong coat in the wrong season will bring about discomfort. As you read this book, take inventory of the coats you have chosen to wear. And by the end of this book you will find yourself a hero by pursuing, adapting, and conquering.

Now we journey into the life of a little boy named Samuel who was given away to live in an unstable environment. He was born into a vow that was made between his mother and God. His mother Hannah, who was unable to bare children prays for a male child and whispers to God a vow that is unheard of. She vows that if God would give her a child she would give him back to HIM. God answers her prayers and she signs the adoption papers, giving the high priest custody to use her son for ministry. What is so surprising to me is that she gets her husband to agree to the deal.

Here we have a couple, considerably upstanding in their community making a decision that appears to the naked eye, insane. How can you finally receive something you've awaited for so long, and then at a given moment give it right back?

I will say this to you. Many times you will pray for something and have other intentions in mind. But God only gives us things that align with HIS will for our lives. Though you may have a certain agenda for the things you pray for, God will in turn give it to you to get it through you. What do I mean? God gave Hannah exactly what she prayed for but then took what she prayed for to do an even greater work for HIS kingdom. You may pray for a car to get you from point A to point B. God blesses you with the car, but you find yourself inviting people to church and picking people up out of generosity. In your mind you're thanking God that you have a way to the grocery store and to run errands, and all the while HE is getting work done for HIS kingdom and receiving the glory from something you've prayed for.

I Samuel 1:17

Samuel's Coat

Now a young child is removed from a stable family and given to an old priest whose discernment is off and his own children are out of control. During this time, the condition of the church was critical. (I Sam 2:12-17). Foreknowing the situation at hand, what parents would knowingly place their child in these conditions?

To ask the question differently, how would Hannah deal with sending off her only child and how would she explain this to her family and friends? More intriguing is the explanation that she had to give to an eight year old that he would no longer live at home with his family, but be sent to live with a half-seeing old prophet. In addition to the prophet who was going blind, he had two sons that were "Priest Pimps!" They not only slept around with the women in the church, they were also stealing from the offering pans. That was a real slap in the face to God huh? You know the statement "Preachers Kids are the worst kids?" Well in this case it was true.

Despite foreknowing the conditions of the contaminated church and its leadership, she enrolled her son into "The Church of the Eyes Wide Shut Tabernacle!" When you think upon it, this is madness. Samuel had two parents who loved him very much. His father Elkaah comes from a lineage of priesthood, and he was financially stable. Elkaah also had another wife with children, giving Samuel brothers and sisters (this was only legal back then).

Hannah enrolled her son into seminary in spite of it. She wanted more for Samuel, by giving up the agenda that she had for him. Like every parent, she probably had his life all mapped out. Remembering the vow she made, Hannah paid the price and made the ultimate sacrifice. Hannah stood fast with the ordained purpose that God had for Samuel's life. This is a true representation of Christ. Hannah gave up her only son just as God did. What are you willing to give up to be like God?

Lesson #1

Hannah made this vow to God and not man. You cannot change your mind about a sacrifice because of the conditions of others. Judging people by the cover is dangerous. Your job is not to judge but to know the voice of the Lord. Hannah had to be familiar with God's voice. Even though she knew the current status of Eli and his household, she did not allow it to sway her from the decision and the vow she made to the Lord.

Lesson #2

Seek the purpose for the things that God gives you. If God knows that he can get something to you to get it through you, you have to become a vessel he can now trust with what he gives to you. God entrusted Hannah with something dear to her heart, her son. And if she could keep a vow of giving up a child she had desperately wanted, then God knew HE could trust her with anything. What can God trust you with that is dear to you?

PART II

I Samuel 1:24

To talk about Samuel and not Hannah would be an injustice. Hannah actively demonstrates "It is better not to make a vow, than to make one and break it." Hannah foreshadows Jesus in her exploit of sending her son to a place of naught, just as God sends Jesus to a place where people have forgotten Him.

Hannah then travels each year to the church to deliver a coat for Samuel without previous measurements. Each year he receives a new

coat, representing several major changes in his life. This also characterizes how we must change coats throughout the course of our lives. To live without growth would be abnormal, if not impossible. Remember, the coat you once wore as a child doesn't fit anymore.
Just as Hannah delivers her son a new coat once a year, you and I can expect God to deliver us a coat every year. The size of the coat is determined on how much you allow yourself to grow. If you outgrow it, GOD is capable of providing you with a coat that gives you time to grow into it. This is how I derived the title "This Coat Doesn't Fit Me Anymore!" Every year Hannah showed up at the church with a new tailor-made coat for her son. It was a spiritual sign that the church has to realize that they have outgrown some traditions and must move on to the next coat that will fit the level of blessing and responsibilities that God has in store.

    Samuel had no say in the choosing of his new home, nor his new godfather. He is now residing on campus, not knowing his purpose. As a child, he's dependent upon his godfather, who is an old preacher. Growing up, Samuel did not have anyone around him his age. He was placed in the temple, and he grew up without the luxury of playing with children his own age. He resided completely in an adult world.

PART III
"I Didn't Ask for This Coat"

    Samuel is a biblical example to all of us who were raised by other people. To all the adopted, abandoned, orphans and foster children who ask the question, "Why me? Why was I given away? Why didn't my parents want me? Why did they choose to raise their other children, and send me on a path that I didn't understand?" This is what the little boy Samuel had to deal with. During this time, Samuel was given a coat that was out of his power.

This coat is also for those who had both parents and those who had only one parent there physically in their life. Many times you can have parents there but they are not there giving you the totality of nourishment that is needed for the proper growth of a child. There are some that are latch-key kids; others are home alone, and then some that are unwanted/unexpected births. Know that when you come into the purpose that God has for your life, you will look back and then see the revelation of why you went through the things you did. And at that moment, you will realize that the anointing God has placed on your life wasn't for you anyway. It was to set someone else free from childhood traumas.

Let me help mend some of your childhood wounds. This coat represents a stage of life that God has ordained for you. Samuel's childhood excluded playing basketball in the backyard with his brothers and his friends. His play time was replaced by learning the books of the bible, and rituals of the church. Do you find your life story somewhere in the bible?

If you think for one moment that you can't get over childhood rejections, you are sadly mistaken. God is in control of your life. You don't have time to grieve over your childhood. Remember that God ordained this coat. God says I'm going to take a messed up childhood and use it for MY glory. How could God allow any child to be given up or taken away from their parents? How could He allow them to be dragged through foster homes? There is a divine purpose for your life. It is not about what you wanted or didn't have. But it is about what you will obtain. Your story will bring life to someone else. The things that you encounter in this life will always minister into the lives of others. And if you're wondering how can I tell you anything, I'm glad you want to know! Before I tell you my childhood experiences, let's briefly return to the story of Samuel.

Samuel
(Teenage Years)

Samuel accepted a new coat from his mother each year. In his eyes it was an ordinary coat, but to the adults of that time, they a new the significance and knew it was a priest's coat. The coats signified that he was next in line to become a high priest.

It doesn't reveal in the scriptures that Samuel was having any problems with his teacher's sons. Maybe because he was too young and naive to understand at that time the Bishop's sons were church pimps.

These ministers had their own agendas. They had an Escort Service in the church and they were married. They openly committed adultery, lied and cheated. Their only concern was money, power and sex. Two thousand years later, the church is still in a battle with this disease, which is a silent killer. No one wants to step up and speak out about these issues that are destroying our lives.

These two ministers didn't fear God. They had no respect for their father's status in the community and no shame in their game. Does this sound familiar to the times in which we live today?

Do you see the example that was set before Samuel? Sex, pollution and corruption was all around him. Maybe as a boy he didn't have a clue, but as a teenager he was surely aware of the corruption going on around him. Surely as his father, the Bishop, heard rumors, he had heard them as well. And the Bishop chose not do anything about it. Oooohhhh!

I Samuel 2:22-25

How did Samuel survive in such a dysfunctional, sinful environment and hold to the coat that was given to him? Could it be he had on the right coat at the right time? Samuel was wearing the appropriate coat for the season for which he was in. Therefore when you are wearing the right coat, it will protect from the corruption that is going on around you. I stress the importance of only wearing the coat God has picked out for you. When you step into a coat designed for someone else, you'll wreak unnecessary havoc on your life. Moreover, it will prolong your time in a season God never wanted you to become stuck in.

The question at hand is what kind of God would allow a child to be raised in that environment? One would also ask, what is God doing? He removes the boy from his Godly parents who appear to have a more stable home, to one that is encompassed with sex, crime and corruption. You see the same reflections or characteristics in the inner city; not to be seen in the church.

Remember that God moves by his own time. He **doesn't sleep or slumber.**

Matthew 13:29-30

The word of God says; "Let the wheat grow up with the tares," meaning let the good grow up with the bad. This young child would be the change for the church and to the nation of Israel. Ezekiel 3:15 says that he sat where they sat. He was able to sit amongst the evil around him and was able to speak proficiently in any situation from a first hand experience. Samuel grew up in this type of environment and became the Senior Prophet. He became the voice that God used to once again open the door of the Prophetic. This coat allowed him to change the position of the church.

Samuel's childhood is a reflection in a mirror for many of us who were given up for adoption. Some of us were given to relatives and some to strangers. I recall at three years of age my sister and I had experienced appalling living conditions. Many times we were left abandoned at home in freezing temperatures. I remember one cold night; I removed the rugs from the floor and covered my 2 year old sister. As I recall, the neighbors came to remove us one very cold night, only to return us to our parents, who struggled with mental issues.

My father served in the Air force in the Vietnam War. Upon his return, he suffered a mental set back. My mother was the valedictorian of her high school class. While she was attending a university, she was thrown a pre-celebration party. They were celebrating her first national television appearance on the Ed Sullivan show.

During this celebration someone poisoned her drink. She was rushed to the hospital and suffered major mental disabilities. Thereafter she was sent back to her small hometown, where she had been honored. She began a long dark journey of alcoholism. She later married my father, and out of this dysfunction she gave birth to my sister and me.

Unmistakably they both came to a decision the weekend of 1960 that they were not equipped for the role of parents. They brought both of us to our grandparent's home for the weekend. We were advised that they were going shopping. One Saturday excursion turned into a lifetime. Subsequently, my mother and father never returned to Florida and they relocated in New Jersey.

After 14 years, my dad finally responded to the letters that my grandparents sent him. During that time my sister was residing with our great Aunt and I remained with our grandparents. I recall watching the door from the couch for many years, waiting for the return of my mother. But just as Samuels life was marked for destiny, so was mine.

There was a period in my life that I experienced rejection. I could not reason with the fact that two educated parents, raised in good Christian homes, would abandon their children. Thus the bitterness began, coupled with fear. After spending cold and dark nights at home alone, I realized that this fear had become a learned behavior and subsequently tortured me through many years of my life.

At that time, I did not know the power of the divine will of God. He eloquently devised a plan and moved it into action, when I was given to my grandparents. To all grandma's kids, this is the strategy of the Almighty God, for you to be raised in a God fearing home. My grandparents were devoted Christians working in ministry. My grandfather was a devout Deacon and my grandmother was a Missionary. Like Samuel, my background mirrors church and more church.

Raised in a Christian home, I shared some of the same experiences of Samuel. I was not able to participate in a lot of activities. By the time I was 14, I made a vow not to be like my mother. Even until this day I have never befriended alcohol, nor participated in any substance abuse. Though I wrestled with unresolved issues, I did not let it stop me from continuing to pursue my dreams.

I entered into high school with the markings of a trendsetter. Being the first black to desegregate the high school sorority clubs, cheerleading and initiating the first girl's basketball team. I was also voted, "Whose Who Among American High School Students." I was also voted the most likely to succeed. Yet I still suffered an underlining void, because I had no one to share in my achievements. My grandparents had entered the age where they were not able to share in my success.

A church girl's perception in life is totally different from those who did not attend church. We always had these questions pondering in our minds. Why can't we go to clubs? Why can't we go to the movies? The theater was forbidden on Sunday, but for teenagers that was the most popular time to hang out. But now I see that it was a shelter of God's divine will. Some teenagers may despise this type of safe haven. In the end you will realize that this is something that God was protecting you from.

I would like to encourage teenagers that you can do it and live out your dreams. Being a dreamer can sometimes lead to name calling as you will see in my next chapter.

I would like to reiterate, in my closing Samuel was raised as an orphan. Through his struggle he became one of the greatest prophets in the Bible. I encourage you to stick to the plan because God's plan is ultimately the plan of success. God's thoughts towards you are thoughts of peace.

Hannah traveled each year to the church, to deliver a coat for her son without previous measurements. Each year he received a new coat which represented new stages of his life. This is symbolic to how we must change coats throughout the course of our lives. The coat you wore as a child must be exchanged. You must go to the coat, which represents the next level of your life and allow yourself room for growth.

Just as Hannah delivers her son a new coat once a year, you can expect God to deliver a coat every year. The size is determined on how much you allow yourself to grow. If you outgrow it, God is capable of giving you something that you will have to grow into. He believes in growth, and he expects it from us.

Samuel's coats represent his prophetic calling and his inauguration into the office of a prophet. Samuel became one of the greatest prophets of his time. From an orphan to a prophet, his story offers hope and comfort for all of us who were given away. Much like myself, I suffered this interval at the age of 3 years old. By unearthing the life of Samuel, it releases me and millions whom subsequently may still have unanswered questions.

I was able to relate and conquer the spirit of rejection and realize that God had destined it to be so from the beginning. God knows our beginning and stands at the end allowing us to apprehend not only His Greatness but His Love for us! It is my prayer that by unveiling details of Samuel's childhood will bring healing to so many unanswered questions to those that sit on our church pews every Sunday and to ones that fill up our local bars.

In reflecting on this chapter, remember that you are wearing the coat that God has designed for your life. Don't stray from the plan. For every coat that Samuel wore there was a reason. His life and the coats he had to wear became a new dawning for the church. You may never know why you go through the things that you go through until the season for that coat has expired. Your experiences are to set some one else free from captivity. Be mindful of the people that are in your presence. They are there for only one reason, and that is because God has put them there.

God placed Samuel in a corrupt environment, not so that he would be subjected into becoming like them, but he was placed there as an example to make the church become more like God. You can do the same on your job, in your church, and in your community!

Chapter 2

Joseph's Coat
Family Drama

Every coat that God has for us isn't always beautiful. Your faith is tested through those you are most susceptible to. Wearing a coat that is placed on you by those who bear the same bloodline isn't always easy. But it is necessary, in order to reach the providence God has prepared.

Jacob, the father of Joseph, had a tailor make him a coat. When Jacob gave Joseph the coat of many colors, havoc reeked amongst the family. Jealousy, envy, hatred and strife began to erupt. The coat did not just represent favor but it also represented a change in leadership and that Joseph would one day lead the tribe of Israel (an interruption of customs). When you're anointed and placed above family members spiritually, naturally it is hard to digest. This was the case with Joseph.

The coat that brought him so much joy would bring a household split, ultimately expelling him from his family.

One of the most outrageous schemes one could imagine was plotted by Joseph's blood brothers to destroy him. All of the scheming and plotting, the hating and jealousy not only riveted over a coat but over a dream as well. Then his brothers use a fictitious death certificate, placing themselves in a position of disbanding Joseph's destiny. "So they thought!" This leads Joseph through countless coat changes.
Let's look at some of the different coats that Joseph had to wear:
Favored Coat: coat of many colors
Slave Coat: sold by his brothers
Butler Coat: house boy
Prison Coat: false imprisonment
Governor's Coat—Promoted to 2nd highest ruler in Egypt.

If he had skipped the fittings of these coats, the promotion of becoming governor would have been a much longer journey. But in Joseph's case, the line up of his coats not only consisted of the beautiful coat of colors, but the coat of betrayal.

It is one thing to be hurt by a best friend and even an associate, but you step into a totally different arena when you're betrayed by family. With friends you can move and find new company, but the bloodline of family keeps you connected even if they despise or disown you. You know the turn you get in your stomach when it's time for family reunion or the days you dread leading up to a funeral? How do you look them in the eye, how do you force a smile? Better yet, how do you keep up a façade around other family members who don't know what happened?

But Joseph demonstrates to us through his life how we all can be healed from family injuries by allowing ourselves to choose forgiveness over harboring bitterness. Again I would like to reiterate that moving forward isn't always easy and never accomplished without a considerable amount of pain.

Joseph's coat reveals the cost of being a chosen vessel out of your daddy's household, associating pain with success. How can you enjoy the success that God has given you when you're in so much pain? Did you not know that often times those two go together? It becomes lonely when you have to enjoy your success alone because you don't have a cheerleading squad to help you celebrate.

Though Joseph's coat of many colors (coat of favor) was ripped and torn off him, his brothers failed to realize that the coat had served its purpose. When Joseph put his arms in that coat, favor saturated him. That is why when they put him in the pit, sold him into slavery and from slavery to prison, everywhere he went, the aroma of favor followed him. When you have the favor of God in your life, you have a supernatural anointing of a magnet. Things begin to draw to you. And guess what - there's nothing you can do about it.

There are many of you whom are reading this book who have suffered various family injuries, from betrayal, family incest, molestation and rape. I will say unto you today, rise up and live and move on. Forgive your family. You're not alone.

Millions of men and women have been inwardly wounded. But we serve a God who is greater than any pain and can turn that pain into a passion to do His will and set others free that have gone through the same situations. But the key phrase is forgiveness. Don't allow the violator to walk around free and you, the victim, become bound and imprisoned in your mind. You've got to let it go and release it into God's hand that you might be free. Now repeat this simple prayer out loud:

Father in the name of Jesus, I release my hurt and the one that hurt me into your hands. I accept this forgiveness today and the power to forgive others in Jesus Name. Selah.

The reappearance of the shadows of your past will resurface and welcome you with open arms. But don't be afraid because Psalm 23 tells us that though we walk through valley of the shadow of death, fear no evil because God is with us. And when God is for us, no one can be against us. That includes the devil! Remember that as shadows fade away, the brighter the light becomes.

How do you shed more light? Through the word of God. Once you begin to meditate day and night, the radiance of the word will began to beam through, arresting the arrogant stance of the shadows.

After twenty years, Joseph has carried his family in his heart but was unprepared to face the message of his pain. The same brothers that had once refused to help him out of a dark, cold pit of death were the same brothers standing before him asking him for help to keep from starving. Looking up and seeing the eyes that withheld hatred and rejection and the contempt trepidation of verbal abuse caused the shadows of the past to appear and the arms of pain embraced him once again.

Can you imagine all of the sleepless nights and the assembly of tears that were shed, the unavoidable nightmares that taunted and awakening in a pool of sweat? This was no easy trial. But he endured because the hand of God was on his life. And there is nothing, and I mean absolutely nothing, that you can't go through and come out ruling like a king when God is your tour guide through the trials of life.

You're the Joseph in your family, you were not chosen so that you can say look what I've accomplished or brag on your riches, how well you can preach or even how good your pronunciation is. But you have been chosen to bring your family out of generation curses, bring them out of the darkness into the marvelous light. God placed his hand on you to be a gateway to bring the rest of your family out of poverty, sickness and disease, bring healing to broken spirits and most of all teach them how to get their name recorded into the Lamb's Book of Life!

The opportunity presented itself for Joseph to seek revenge. When his brothers stood in his midst, he had to hide himself and cry. Though the wound had healed, it still hurt. Forgiveness is the best medicine for the pain of the past. When nothing else can help, just try it and watch how fast the results of healing will manifest. And because he chooses forgiveness versus bitterness, millions of lives were spared.

This coat symbolically represents the changes and phases one would go through. Each Christian must realize there will be drama in our lives. This phase also represents how family will become jealous over your coat. If you want my coat, you must know my story. It also reveals how one can have many talents. The body of Christ must realize the power that we possess nothing of our own but of God. This coat was given to you by your father. You didn't ask for it. Maybe in the eyes of others, you don't deserve it.

What jealous folks don't realize is that the coats that God issues are not free of charge. There will always be a price to pay. Love comes with a high price tag. That coat almost cost Joseph his life. Because he was not Christ, his death would not have been necessary because his blood could not have saved us from our sins. But his life is a similitude of Christ.

Do people love you for what you have or do they love the character of GOD that is displayed within you. The God in you will attract people to you because of His love that is within you and it makes people want to be around you and they don't even know why. Through this, God can express His love and cause His glory to be revealed. Remember these different coats are not for you but for God to receive the glory. That's why you can't hold on to them. Allow the God to pass you your next coat. Who said that you had to keep that coat just because your daddy gave it to you?

Sometimes when you are called out from your family, they can't comprehend because to them you are just lil sis or lil Johnny. Jesus said many are called, but few are chosen. Jesus Himself suffered rejection from his family and His community in which He grew up. Jesus recognized His divine calling and purpose, which He eloquently fulfilled. Joseph was called out to ultimately save his family and an entire nation. Some of you who are reading this chapter may not understand why you had to be disconnected from your family.

My suggested theory is that you are in the middle of process, in order to fulfill your divine purpose. Allow the testimony of Jesus to comfort you. His brothers and sisters at first could not accept His mission. Instead of acknowledging who He was, they insisted on calling Him the carpenter's Son (Isn't that Mary's Boy). Some people will never accept your calling and therefore you may experience loneliness. For example, personally when He called me and anointed me in the priesthood, He called me out from my family and church and relocated me to another city.

Relocating can cause separation among family and friends. We see the same pattern when God called Abraham out from his family. (Sometimes is it the inseam of the coat; which is your family or those that are connected closer to you). It was for him to fulfill his divine purpose. Separation can often be misunderstood because of the plan of God. Sometimes God has to break that co-dependency, move all the crutches. His purpose is that you may learn Him for yourself, in retrospect, when he calls you; you will be prepared to answer him. He de-programs to reprogram so that you can fulfill your destiny.

Coats weren't made to last for ever! With no limitations, Joseph became one of the most power men of his time because of the principle of forgiveness. Not wearing the coat his natural father made, but he wore the one that was tailor made by God, which is far greater than any human could create with such a perfect fit.

I would like to announce to you that your time has arrived. It's time for you to move on and moving on can sometimes cause major delays because of fear. Because of fear, moving into a place of new direction, a place of unfamiliarity can cause a person to pull back from the plan of God. Your mind puts up a shield blocker and the scenes of past failures, childhood hurts and unexpected traumas. Just take the tape out and replace it with God's instructional DVD. Once you begin, view and rehearse over and over the blueprints that God has laid out for your life and the scenes of that old life will begin to fade away, like a pair of old blue jeans.

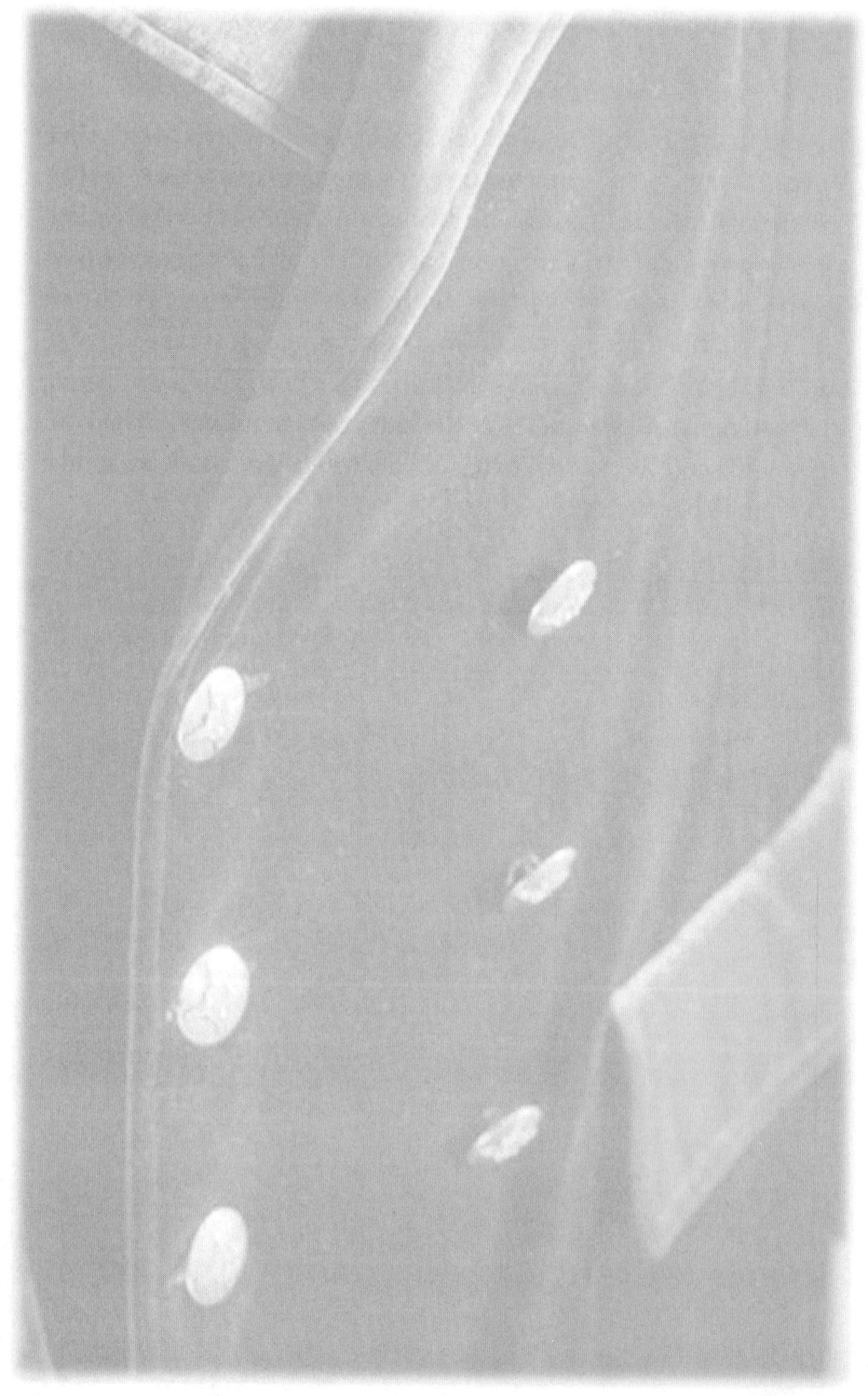

Chapter 3

Your Coat Doesn't Fit Me

There are battles we face that are unavoidable. But we must face them knowing that with God on our side all things are possible. Make sure that you acquire knowledge for the battle. Facing adversity with strategy is always wise. Remember that the giants that we face are equipped to take us down and wipe us out. But when you're wearing your coat and not someone else's, then you've won the battle and war without exerting your own strength.

Sometimes we are seen through the eyes of others as incapable of mastering the task set before us. And because of their great accolades and fame they've received, they feel arrogant and want to tell you how the job should be done. Isn't it funny how people can advise you on a job or situation that they couldn't get done themselves? That's like a dog trying to teach a cat how to meow!

A young man in the Bible by the name of David is called into the house one afternoon by his father. His father wants him to take a trip to the battlefield to take food to his older brothers. Upon obeying his father, he arrives at the war only to discover that the giant named Goliath is mocking Israel's military. David becomes more and more offended as he listens to the giant insulting the God of Israel. Immediately he requests to see the Chief Commander, King Saul. He receives his clearance and goes before the King. David clears his throat, and he gives his qualifications to fight this giant. He mentions the night he was tending to his father's sheep, a bear and a lion came to eat one of the sheep and he killed them with his bare hands. In this testimony, David reveals that he has obtained favor and an unusual anointing upon his life. God has given him power that is beyond human strength.

After David finishes his address, the entire room that was once filled with laughter because of his size drafts a thick aroma of silence. King Saul arises and affirms David. The King is convinced that he is capable of conquering the giant. The King offers his strategy on how to approach this giant and requests for him to wear his coat of armor. He also recognizes David's anointing but tells him how his battle with the lion and bear does not compare to the giant. He says to David that no one has been able to defeat the giant, not even an entire army.

David allows the king to dress him in his armor but quickly realizes that the coat doesn't fit. It's too big! David boldly confesses that this coat doesn't fit and David tells the King that his weapons are foreign to him as well.

David's confession that the coat didn't fit is a spoken word to us today. There can only be one outcome when we allow other people to push us out before our time and do things that are beyond our human and spiritual level of strength. You become a casualty to the kingdom of God. God will put no more on you than you can bear. You go beyond the strength that God has graced you when you leave yourself uncovered and leave yourself as an open target for the enemy. Only coats that are made by God have a custom fit. One must be tested and proven to be capable of moving to the next level.

In school before taking the next assignment, you must be successful in the first one. We need to be trained and equipped for the tasks that God has allotted to us. As a Pastor, I have observed a myriad of people who run to the pulpit to preach. However they have not had proper assessments to qualify them for the call of duty as a preacher. Preachers are not hired but called by God. If you take a job without applying, you will eventually be found out and fired. And it is the same with God. If you allow people to push you to preach, God will eventually find you out and He's more powerful than Donald Trump in the "Apprentice." You will be fired but judged at a higher cost.

The most powerful man of that time offered David his coat. But David refused because he understood that he was not worthy to wear such a coat. You can play the part and put on a wonderful façade but you're playing a very dangerous game. Using what works for others may not work for you. Everyone must learn the lesson that admiring people's power and influence should never be the basis for putting on an unassigned coat.

David told the king that he would use what he had and that was the faith that God gave him. I must point out that we are to attain our own faith and our teacher. God is watching to see if you are arrogant and full of pride. God wants to see if we will try to do things out of our own power. In this event it only proves to Him that we need a little more experience under our belt, to teach us that we can't do anything without His approval, grace, and power.

I'm quite sure you can recall going through certain things over and over again. Well let me turn your light bulb on. You keep getting an "F" on the test and will until you complete it by putting on the coat. You will be assigned to take the test again, and prepare to take out pen and paper and take it again!

David now approaches the battlefield with his God given experience, the only coat that he'll need to win. He went with his own anointing, and his own experiences.

David took his staff and chose 5 smooth stones and moved towards the giant. Tell your friends that you thank them for being there, but you must fight your own battles. But you have to fight this fight the way that you know how. You know there are some people that can talk their way out fights by talking a lot of noise. I'm a perfect example. In school I wasn't the one to talk a lot of trash. If you told me you were going meet me after school at dumpsters, you would be waiting until nightfall. Because while you're in your last class, I would get permission from the office to leave early and while you're waiting to put a couple of knots on my head, I was home with my grandmother watching the soap operas! Then the next day in school in the cafeteria I would brag about I was there early, where were you. What I really was saying was I was there in spirit but not my flesh!

I'm trying to paint a clear picture for you. David was really saying in our terms, "I can't fight with your stuff; I can't fight how you fight!" Example: you say "I wish I was in her shoes," not knowing her happiness is just a show. Or you look at a couple and say to yourself, "I wish my marriage was like their marriage." And at home there is infidelity and abuse taking place. The scripture says, "One that compares oneself to another is not wise." Food for thought huh?

Back to the story. David takes the armor off and says, "I can't wear this." It demonstrates to the church that he had to fight the devil the way God had equipped him. Some people can talk their way out." Some people pray their way out. Some people are so smooth that they quietly ease their way out.

It is now 14 years after David refused the king's coat. But something had to happen before he could put on a coat of that magnitude. When God tells you to wait, wait doesn't mean never. If I could open your brain, I would slam-dunk it in there. Fourteen years later David is the same man but of a different stature. He's been running for 14 years with an anointing. Samuel the prophet has anointed him to become king and David had to wait for 14 years. Meanwhile he has been running from Saul. The same man that invited David to the palace and welcomed him into the family was the same one plotting to kill David. But I'm assured that David was not sitting by the dock of the bay wasting time. David was running for his life. What do you do when someone offers you a position and then turns on you? What do you do when you buy the house and it goes into foreclosure or you buy the car and it gets repossessed? I'll tell you what you need to do; you need to keep on moving. You can't just stand there and die!

One of David's personal trials took place when David and his men came into Ziglag. They found their homes burned down and the women and children taken captive. David had a family but he was in an unstable condition. I know that there are men reading this book that are tired of living unstable and beneath their heritage. Or you may have lost your family just as David had. Well I want to tell you in spite of losing materialistic things or losing your family, it ain't over. I know that's not correct English. But "IT AIN'T OVER! Your God has heard your cry, because righteous prayer availeth much. What do you do when you've been bringing the rent money home, and paying the bills on time and it still isn't enough? I'll tell you, stand still with your loins girded about. If God allows you to be broke or allows you to be down and out, know that that coat is too small and He has another one for you.

David and the men that were with him lifted up their voices and wept until they had no more power to weep. David was greatly distressed for the men spoke of stoning him because the souls of the men were grieved. They thought of killing David. And like David, you have to encourage yourself. Sometimes you're with people who won't encourage you but yet celebrate when you're going through. You've been delayed by dumb folks. They can see success written across you forehead.

David's back is completely against the wall. David calls for the high priest and requests his priestly robe. This coat has 6 stones on each side that represent the 12 tribes of Israel. Each name of the 12 tribes was listed on the stones. Why were the stones put on the coat? When the high priest put the coat on and entered into the holy of holies, God would look upon the 12 stones and remember the children of Israel. It was a sacred coat and it was only to be worn to seek God. And the only person that could put the coat on was the high priest at that time. But by the time it trickled down to David's time, there was no high priest to go before God. Why? Because they were all dead except for Abithar.

Abithar finds David and hooks up with him. I would say, "You need to be connected to someone who's able to relate to what you are going through." Mark the person who gains without experience. They won't appreciate it; they will turn and spit in your face.

Now David tells Abithar to bring the coat. David is not considered a priest, but he tells the priest to bring him the coat. You better stop waiting for the priest to come and pray your family through. Become like David and say, "I need that coat; I have got to go to God for myself."

Now in studying the life of David, it has taught me some important facts. God has given us another opportunity. David said we can go to God for ourselves. David had an emergency. His family was gone and his friends wanted to kill him. Yet through the grief he was suffering, he had to make a choice. He had to go pray for himself. There was no family or friends there to touch and agree, no prayer line he could call upon, nor a priest in a booth to whom he could speak. He had to pray on his own. He entered into the church and he lay prostrate before God and prayed and didn't move until he heard from God.

Here is where the problem lies in the church. We become restless and often we don't have time to wait on God. Therefore we move out of emotions instead of being led by God. We turn to others for advice and some people mean well but there are some things that only God can solve. We must go to God for ourselves.

David's life impressed me so much that I have tried to pattern my life around his testimonies. He taught me what it means to know God for myself. In viewing his life, I have learned to wait on what God has for me and how to seek to please God. No matter what task I may face, if I trust God, he will answer.

David prayed in faith and God not only answered him but God told David that he shall recover all. After this trial, David was now empowered with the anointing for the next level in his life, and that was being appointed King. He so profoundly demonstrated to us how to wait for the right time and use what God had already given us.

And in using what God has given you, the test is passed and you can move to the next level.

My dear friend, I hope that after reading this chapter you will boldly take a stand. If it doesn't fit, don't force it. God has created you for His divine purpose, so wearing someone else's coat and imitating someone is an insult to God. God signs his own labels and when he made you, you were made in a fabulous design, a designer's original.

Chapter 4

The Political Coat

I King 3:5

Some coats that God places on you come with Political Power. There are many that are given these coats and abuse it. The handling of coats with Political Power must be done with precision, as if you were handling a bomb. A Political Power coat that explodes will not only damage you, but it will have more effect on those that are placed under your leadership.

The chronicle begins with Solomon. He has been given a political coat. During this era, King Solomon was very young. The Bible doesn't tell us his age at the time of this coat change. Some theologians disclose that he was in his early thirties. He takes the position of his father, King David and his coat changes from being a prince to a king.

He is now inaugurated as king and he takes a position that his father carried. His father had a reputation insomuch that the people in the City stated, "When David Speaks, God Speaks." With such an astounding reputation of his father, this made it hard for Solomon to walk in his footsteps.

Solomon returns from the temple after the inauguration and goes to bed. It's a good feeling knowing that you've done the right thing. Many times we say and do the wrong things and go to bed and can't sleep. But in Solomon's case, he has done the right thing, therefore giving him not only a night of peaceful sleep, but he has a dream that changed the course of his life. His actions had pleased God insomuch that God showed up surreal in his dream.

As soon as Solomon receives his new coat, the very next day he is put to test. He judges his first case, which involves a murder of an infant. The case consists of two harlots that were roommates. On that dreadful night, one rolls over and smothers her baby. After she realizes she has killed her baby, she then switches her dead baby with her roommates, to make the presumption to the other woman that the dead baby belongs to her. They both present astonishing cases. After both parties have been heard, King Solomon has to make a ruling. He uses such profound wisdom that it exceeds that of natural thinking. This case was so extraordinary in its time that his name began to circulate throughout kingdoms far and wide because of his great wisdom.

At that time Solomon understands that he received his gift of wisdom from God. He was considered a political giant to his comrades. But his greatness in power and wisdom quickly became his downfall. Sometimes worldwide fame can lead to a path of self-destruction. Fame can become like lights to a deer. It blinds you to where you only see a reflection of self and fail to realize that God gave you the status that you obtained.

Solomon was exposed to so much power, fame and wealth at such a young age that arrogance became his coat. We can reach a prominence in the corporate world and the church that we become untouchable and unaccountable for our actions. And without accountability, one will steer into a utopia of contamination without self-acknowledgment of wrongdoings.

Solomon no longer depended upon God for wisdom, but now operated from his own will. Self-destruction crept into his corridor and it is here that he began to tread on unstable waters. A man that is left to govern himself is an accident waiting to happen. Solomon is a prime example that money doesn't make you intelligent. However, it makes you susceptible to making mistakes that not only affect you, but those close to you. There is such as thing as a poor fool as well as a rich one.

Instead of following in his father's footsteps, Solomon chose an uncultivated road of obsession. He became obsessed with his wisdom, women and power. And with the power that was at his disposal, he devoured the kingdom that his Father had built upon the ways of God.

History repeats itself today among our leadership. From the church house to the White House we see a trend of power abuse. People take this power and use it for self-advantage. They use it to manipulate men and women into their spider webs of immorality. Instead of the money being spent on charity and improvement of our communities, it is used on hotels, cars, extravagant gifts for lovers, and has turned the house of God into a penthouse of sin.

Jesus said that many people are destroyed by the lack of knowledge. We often times put our trust in our leaders set before us and drift from the devised plan of God. Your dependency should never be upon leaders but always to God. At times the coat of power blinds us. And the light from the coat of power is so blinding that to the naked eye the sin within the coat is oblivious.

Sin is always wrong even when introduced by leadership. If you're ever approached in this manner, quickly run in the opposite direction. There are thousands of men and women bleeding from leaders who are upheld in the utmost adoration but their coat is dirty.

There is a solution and it begins with repentance and acknowledging that one needs help. The assumption that one can have the best of both worlds will no longer be tolerated. Eventually you will have to choose one coat, either the coat of Righteousness or the Coat of Destruction. Because sin will take you further than you want to go, and make you pay a price higher than you want to pay. The price of choosing self-will is a costly coat because sin has a higher price tag. But when you choose a coat tailored by God, it's free of charge because of the ultimate sacrifice He's already paid. For the wages of sin is death, but the gift of God is eternal life.

The political coat was written to pull the covers back and bring the spotlight on and ongoing problem. As we watch history replay itself, the White House, the church house needs a fresh new start. Corruption has contaminated leadership in both arenas, political and spiritual. There has to be a demand put on today's leadership. A call for clean, honest and God fearing leaders with integrity and accountability. The silence must be broken. It is indeed sending the wrong message to our next generation. Power and position don't authenticate that one can live a life full of riches and fame.

Both politician and pastors have taken an oath. That oath was to lead the people and not cause the people to bleed. They also vowed to serve in the public arena, as a public servant. What is the meaning of a servant?

I speak from an audience that is tired of disappointment by leadership. We are like toddlers, who get tired of baby food, push it away and spit it out.

We want change, and we want it now. I believe we must put a demand on our government as well as our Christian leadership. There has to be a new campaign and have Jesus as the campaign manger. The word of God says that if His people who call His name will humble themselves and seek His face and turn from their wicked ways, He will hear them and heal their land. In the days of old, God played a very strong role in government. A man or a woman could not hold a political office without the ordination of God. First and foremost God selected who was placed in the White House as well as the church house. Election is dangerous when it is controlled by the wrong person.

I am calling for a new mandate. This is a new century and it is time for change. In the process, God will start exposing the coat. In the gospel of Matthew, He said, "The ax is being laid at the root of the tree", Jesus warns us through the writing of Apostle Paul that in the last days there will come a great falling away from the church. But he quickly reminds us not to be shaken.

The Apostle Paul reminds us again in his writing in the book of Timothy 3, that in the last days men would become lovers of there own flesh: headed, ignorant, controlling, proud and denouncing the power of God and allowing themselves to become demoralized. They are living a contaminated and erroneous life style, engaging in an adultery, fornication and homosexual life style.

Then they choose to down play their own hearts, and allude to a Holy God, who they blame for making them that way. I strongly feel if you are going to engage in this sinful lifestyle, come on out with the truth - step up to the plate, and admit this is a choice and stop trying to compare the civil rights, blacks and Jews. In order to be healed, one must first realize that he is in trouble. We must be careful in the choices that we have made in doing so; we send the wrong message to those that are followers.

If by chance you are blessed to serve as a Christian Leader, these positions should be entered into with sincerity and integrity. Often times in the beginning stages, most leaders serve well. But as years progress the purpose and oath that was taken, somehow become minute and often forgotten. God is a jealous father and overprotective fathers can become upset when all that they have given has become unappreciated. At the same time, He is forgiving and always allows room for one to correct his or her actions.

As we glance into the life of King Solomon, (the son of King David), we see a man extremely overtaken with pride, money and sex. Such as our society today, we see the same pattern replicated. It is as the old saying goes, "Don't forget the bridge that brought you over." And that same ladder that you climbed to realm of success will be the same one that will take you back down to reality when you misrepresent God. And remember that coming down the ladder isn't as easy as going up.

King Solomon started his journey with such a humble path, insomuch that God told him to ask Him for anything he wanted. And Solomon's response did not consist of materialistic desires, but of all things he asked for wisdom. His wish was granted and he became one of the wisest and wealthiest men of all time. But as most people, Solomon deviated from the original blueprints. God was no longer the center of his attention but money, power and sex became the arena he dwelled in. God will raise up individuals and he can bring them down. He can open doors just as He can close them. God is patient and longsuffering but if you will not repent then his judgment will find its way to you. As Christians we are expected to illustrate morals and good character, especially as Pastors and Politicians. God is expecting us to follow guidelines and not abuse the power He has given us. When the opportunity presents itself, take the time to think about what sacrifices, the self discipline, hardship and faithfulness it took just to get to where you are. Let's take a moment of silence and think…

O.K. now did you not know that it is going to take that and much more just to maintain and increase?

As we've seen for many years, a man in power is within arms reach of anything and everything imaginable. But there is a great change that God is bringing within the political arena. God is watching over our government and He is never surprised by who is elected. Just as He watched over the nations thousands of years ago, He's still watching. And Kings who abused their power and led the country into sin and unrighteous He brought forth public embarrassment.

God is going to clean up every political arena from Democrat to Republican and all the in-betweens. This country was founded on Godly principals. And those in office, may think because they have power that they can make life altering decisions because they may feel certain laws and constitutes don't fit into this new millennium. But God will always have the last say so. The power does not belong to them, it was only loaned out. And when power is not handled properly, interest will be added to the debt owed by you and me. And God's math is not like ours.

Our churches are experiencing a purging. And no denomination is exempt. Ministers of the Gospel will be judged according to their own sins as well as those in office. Sin is sin in God's eyes, from the White House to the Crack House, from the Pulpit to the Door.

Becoming a leader should be approached with caution and handled with care. Just as in the corporate world, when the managers are not doing their jobs and mishandling authority, it will find them out and the blame will not be upon those in which they are over. God is in search of God fearing men and women to raise up and establish in power. I encourage you to observe your children carefully because they may be the next candidate for a political office or the next spiritual leader.

In this chapter God wanted me to alert readers of three things to keep in mind;

1. God does watch over the state of the government as well as the church.

2. God doesn't have a problem with riches but how it's obtained and how it's being used.

3. God does not want anyone to forget that He is the one that anointed you for a position of power.

God does not want your end to be like Solomon. Because of the power Solomon obtained, it drew woman from far and near. It made him accessible to anything that he wanted. Solomon became involved with women who worshipped idol gods and committed lewd and immoral acts. Solomon began to display himself very loosely and improperly. And because of it, he strayed away from the foundation that had been molded by his father King David. It also cost him his kingship. God will not tolerate leadership that will lead His people away from Him. In comparison many of our political leaders past and present have aborted the mission of God's precepts and have and will be exposed publicly. I'm quite sure several come to mind!

But once again I stress the importance of taking a position of leadership and not willing to make the sacrifice of showing integrity, humility, and responsibility. Many forget that whatever office you're put in it is to serve, not to be served. And money and power have somehow blinded the call of duty. Be aware of taking positions and money that will cause you to agitate God, because God said, "Don't offend even the little ones." And can I make a statement that is needed upon hiring any and everyone? Be honest to yourself, if you are not a people person and not willing to serve with compassion, respect, and integrity, leave public relations alone. You not only have a obligation to the people you serve but to the God you serve. Let's wear these coats demonstrating to God and man that you have the best of both worlds, remaining with integrity and the character of God.

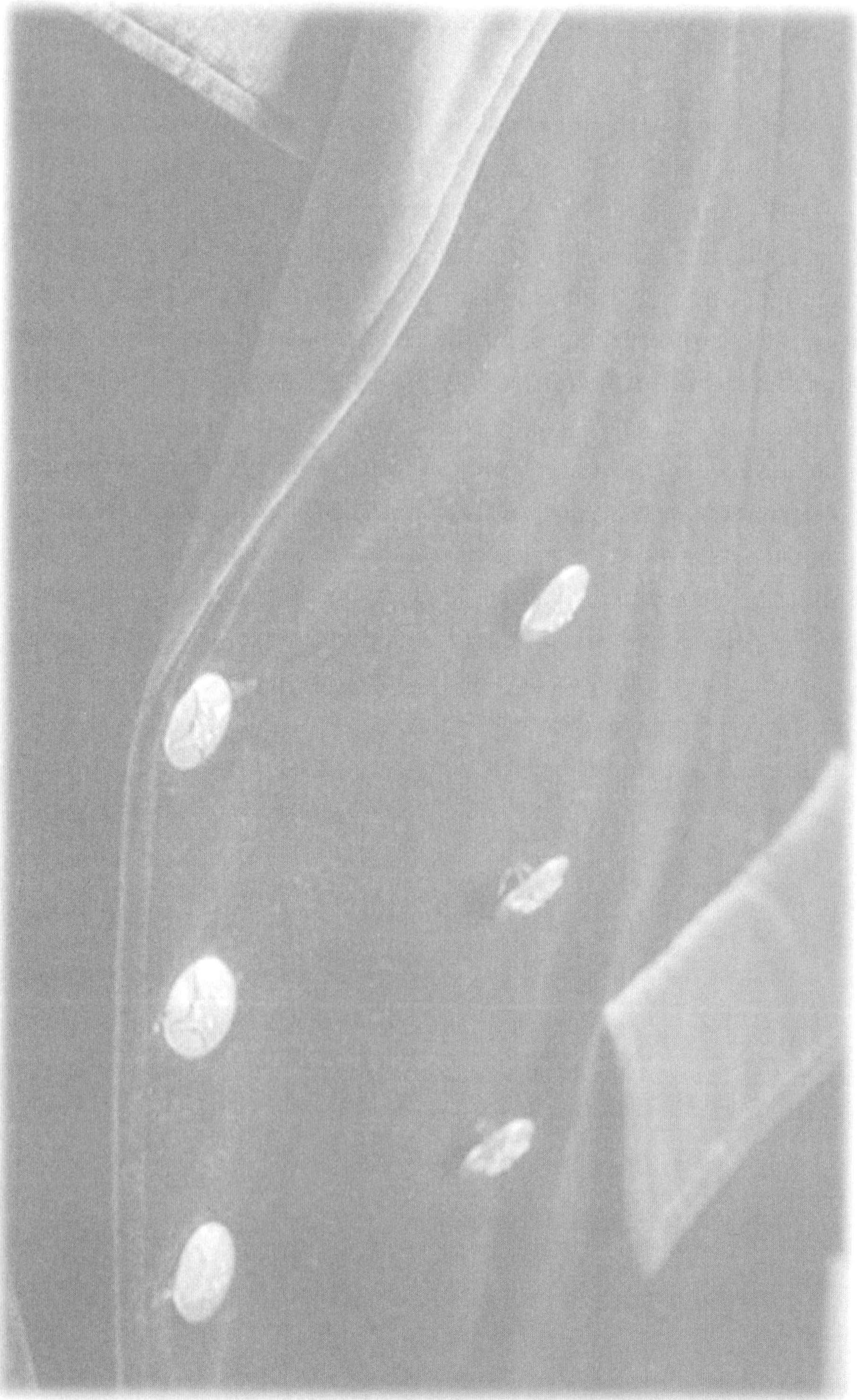

Chapter 5

The Prophetic Coat

The Need for Mentorship and Impartation

This chapter deals with the definitive need for mentorship and impartation. There is a daily need for training and mentorship in today's society. When God has given you a talent and gifts, it is imperative that you receive proper guidance or you will misconstrue the purpose of these gifts and misuse them. Lets look into the life of a young candidate when destiny knocks on the door.

Elisha was a young man who was tending to his father's fields. Then Elijah, the Senior Prophet, comes with an anointing to do the will of the Lord. Elijah was Elisha's teacher. Elijah helped mentor Elisha in the right direction. When God gives you a coat and the wrong person is teaching you the purpose of that coat, this can become a disaster. The disaster evolves about when you take a coat that is made for summer and wear it in the winter; for example, people that are psychics. God has given them gifts. But somewhere down the line they were mentored in the wrong way. They were given those gifts to be used in the kingdom of God and not to make money for selfish gain. Therefore they are wearing their coat that God has given to them the wrong way because of misguidance.

God enrolled Elisha in a prophetic school, which was very important. The greatest Senior Prophet, Elijah, trained him. I emphasize the need for spiritual teachers as well as natural teachers. Elijah was the CEO and Founder of the Prophetic Seminary.

In this chapter of the prophetic coat, I discuss Elisha's first semester of prophetic school. Elijah was the CEO of the Prophetic Seminary in which God enrolled Elisha. Elisha learned how to be a caregiver by serving his teacher and learned the purpose of his prophetic calling. An epidemic in churches today is that we have Peter-Pan prophets flying around without being trained or mentored. They're living in Neverland without realizing the magnitude of their JUDGEMENT, and saying what God did not say. It begins with a lack of understanding and accountability. You cannot be elected to this office; it is a higher calling, only to be chosen by God.

Let's study how Elisha, the student, was willing to wait for his training. His first semester was learning how to become a servant to the teacher. It is very important to have mentorship in our lives. We should learn how to wait for the proper training, so that we can learn how to utilize these gifts that have been passed on by God. Many people have callings, but they lack understanding of the operations of the gift.

Some of you may not even know what a prophet and prophetess is. A prophet or prophetess is a male or female who speaks on the behalf of God revealing past, present, and future, as well as warnings, judgements and demonstrating works of miracles and healings.

The Bible reveals in the book of Amos that God will do nothing until he reveals it to his prophets first. In the days of old, a prophet was called a seer. If a person needed directions from God, he or she would travel near and far to see a prophet. That prophet would then minister to him the word of the Lord. Many people wear these titles today. Jesus said his people are destroyed because of the lack of knowledge. They have brought confusion to the hearts of people because of their lack of training and self-appointment. This has become a widespread misconception. Like any other gift, prophets are birthed and called by God.

But mostly what you tend to see demonstrated is self promotion from those who disguise themselves as being called of God. Then they say things that God didn't say. The Bible warns of such practices. God says, "Woe unto the man who says, and God has not spoken."

The office of a prophet can be found in the book of Ephesians 4:11-13. If by chance you have had some experience or sense you have this calling, you should find a church or a mentor who operates in that gift. You need guidance and leadership from one who is currently operating in that gift. For example, if you want to become a doctor or perfect the knowledge you already have as a doctor, you don't attend cosmetology school. In all gifts and offices, God wants us to learn how to serve and how to be served.

This gift is sought after more than any other gift in the Bible. One reason people desire this position is because they feel power in knowing people are dependant upon them to reveal what the future has in store. And then there are those who prey on people who are weak and vulnerable. Jesus told us to know them that labor among you. In other words, know the people that you surround yourself with spiritually as well as physically. BE MINDFUL OF STRANGERS! But be reassured that when God calls you, He will place His seal of approval and set you out above men. People will recognize your fruit and God's word will not return unto him void. In God there is safety and He will allow you to cross paths with someone to help you activate your gift, just as he did with Elisha and Elijah.

The Prophetic Coat

Let's take an in depth look into the wearing of Elisha prophetic coat. In the timing of this text, Elijah the teacher, was approaching the end of his season and Elisha is in the church with no position, getting ready to have a destiny collision. There are so many of us in church on the wrong path. And upon taking the wrong paths we have collisions with the wrong things. Therefore when we collide with the wrong things, it gives us a setback and the recovery is painstaking. But once you take the right path that God has chosen for your life, you'll experience spiritual accidents that were purposely set in place for you. Spiritual accidents are always beneficial, valuable, and life changing.

The Bible states one day to the Lord is like a thousand years and a thousand years is like but one day to Him. What you think will take years to happen will only take seconds for God. Before the foundation of the world, God had already signed an overnight package to be delivered on a specified date for your life - just as he did for Elijah. Little did Elisha know, he was preparing for a job and his time card had already been created.

On the other hand, Elijah the teacher was coming to the close of his season. "To everything there is a time and a season." Elijah the teacher was persevering personal struggles of his own. But through all of this, God had called him on a new assignment. What do you do when duty calls and you don't have the strength to proceed or follow through with the instructions. God's plan cannot be stopped by the trials in your life. Elijah was burnt out, tired and extremely depressed and in that devastated condition he went to hide in a cave to prepare himself for suicide. He had no food, no weapons, and he was alone. Elijah, without an announcement to his staff, got up and left. Being a leader he felt that there was no one that he could talk to or confide in regarding what he was going through. Often times as a leader you look around at your staff and you feel they can't relate to your problems. The reality of it all is that there are people that you work with, live with and socialize with who don't realize you're about to explode and cause a drastic disaster. And because of past failures, it hinders you from moving forward or causes you hide in a cave like Elijah.

Oftentimes we stay shackled to our past and frightened of our future, leaving our present unattended. That leaves our current situation to reek havoc, and because we are living in the past, we haven't a clue on how to handle the present. But I speak as a Prophetess of the Lord to you this very moment. Splash some cold water on your face, put on your game face and look your past directly in the eye and command it to be exactly what it is, "your past." Your past is meant to stay behind you, not block your view of the future. Sometimes when you are driving down the road, there's a car in your blind spot and as you try to get over, without warning or a honking of the horn, it runs into you and you never saw it coming. Our past operates the same way. When we try to enhance our spiritual lives, we look in our rear view mirrors at our past and see nothing. And the moment we take that next step or that promotion or go to the next level, here comes your past out of nowhere and it causes a "ten year" pile up.

We all know that there are things in our past that we cannot make disappear. But wise up and use it to your advantage. God's word said that all things work together for the "good" of those who love God. And no matter how devastating or how altering your past may have been, it doesn't change how God thinks about you because his thoughts of you are good. And if you have confidence in the our God Jehovah, you will begin to see what you've been through clears a path, revealing the anointing, prosperity and peace that God has waiting. You are a child of the most high and of the royal priesthood and a glass ceiling isn't strong enough to hold you captive. How many Kings Kids do you know that spend their royal lives in a dungeon?

But in the midst of Elijah pulling the plug to his own life support, God steps in. Thank God that His eyes are all seeing and He doesn't look at our position. God monitors his children. He can show up in the strangest places to find you, because your destiny is too costly to allow it to be destroyed. God showed up where Elijah was hiding in the cave. God can find you no matter where you think you're hiding. Like many of you, if you stay in hiding you think you will not be held responsible for fulfilling the assignment God has given you. But just like God showed up in the cave, He will show up where you are. God didn't just show up but he came with restoration, healing, refreshing, and strength for Elijah to complete the assignment.

A Day of the Unexpected

Time has passed since Elisha first caught his coat and he's still a student, but he senses another change is coming. Do you sense that your coat is about to change? You've been doing very well as an usher, as a greeter, or as good steward over God's money. Elisha has had time to serve under a leader, and the time has come when the student must be promoted to Senior Prophet. Elijah's time was up and it was time to pass the coat. Catch this while you're reading this book. God is in the pitching position. He's saying, "Next batter come to the plate!" Are you ready?

Elisha is now ready to be promoted but he can't go without a coat. I'm tired of seeing people who call themselves prophets and apostles and every other name and don't have a coat. So whatever you do, wait for the coat!" Isaiah said, "Those that wait shall mount as with wings of eagles." There is strength already in place for you to do the will of the Lord. It's time for you to catch this coat.

Elijah went from city to city before Elisha could receive the coat. This represents that there are many journeys that you will take before you reach your destination of receiving the coat that God has for you. When we were young, there were times that we would try on our parent's clothes and they were too big. We anxiously awaited the time when we would be able to fit into them perfectly. But we had to do the accurate things in order to grow. The same goes for the spiritual. You must be meticulous in what you feed your spirit, in order for it to grow. Now if you plant tomatoes, you're going to get tomatoes. So whatever you plant into your spirit, that is what you will see produced.

The Transfer

So Elisha is ready for promotion but his classmates are not. His fellow students, fifty in all, began to tell him that his master was going to be taken away. And he answered, "Yes I know, so hold your peace." Then the students began to stand afar to see what was going to take place. There are times in our lives when God will allow people that are close to you to stand afar because he doesn't want any contamination in the flow of what He's getting ready to do in your life. He doesn't want them speaking into your ear, because your ear is a doorway to your soul, and you have to be careful of what you hear in the time of your promotion.

Elijah took his mantle (coat), wrapped it together and smote the waters of Jordan and He and Elisha walked over on dry ground. I don't know about you, but I've had a raincoat, I own a winter coat, I wear sports coat, but none of them are the appropriate coat to lead me to the other side where God has my destiny mapped out.

Now this is the part I really like about this story. The Bible says that Elijah asked Elisha, "What is that you will have me to do?" Elisha answered, "I want a double portion of your spirit." Then Elijah said it shall be yours. And as they talked, a chariot of fire showed up like a whirlwind. If Elisha had not been familiar with the anointing, it would have frightened him. But because he had spent years with the prophet of God who operated in the anointing of God, he was in the receiving mode. Remember that folks will always try to hinder you. While folks are talking about you, and calling you everything low down and good for nothing, God is going to show up like a whirlwind. As people say your season is over and God has left you, I'm here to tell you that talk has never changed God's mind about you. So many times we give power to people, and we believe that one man's negative words against us are going to stop opportunity. Heed my words, that whatever they say about you, keep your eyes on the master, just as Elisha did.

As they were talking, Elijah's ride showed up in a whirlwind. How in the world can a man stay on the ground in a whirlwind? Now technically a whirlwind is just another word for a tornado. How could Elisha just stand there when a whirlwind was right in front of him? During disasters we have to tape our windows, board them up and go to our basements or the smallest room of our houses. With all of that wind and fire that took Elijah up, how come it didn't take Elisha up as well. But because it was appointed for Elijah, that wind that came was not coming against him but for him. And the only thing that moved was Elijah's clothing that was left behind. I would like to interview a meteorologist and see what answers they could provide. I don't know about you but at this point in my life if my clothes are going to be the only thing that I lose, I believe I'll run on and see what the end is going to be. If it costs me some friendships, a house or car, I believe it will be worth it in the end, to see the abundance that God has for me.

How come Elijah didn't reach back and grab his clothes when they fell off. No one wants to be naked. Could it be the same reason Jesus didn't reach for his when they took his? The Bible says the soldiers reached up and snatched his garment off him. Jesus had all power; he could have reached and grabbed his clothes back. But He knew the same clothes that God clothed Him with on the day of transfiguration and He knew same power still existed.

Let's continue. The Bible says that while Elijah was caught up, Elisha stood right there. Elisha saw it and cried, "My Father, my Father." And after he saw Elijah no more, Elisha took off his clothes and tore them in half. You're about to move some things out your closet. You're about to separate yourself from some of the things you once had. Now stand still until the storm is over. Don't be moved by the situations around you.

Elisha reaches down and takes up Elijah's coat and goes back to the bank of Jordan and takes the coat and smites the water and says, "Where is the Lord God of Elijah?" What you must understand is that he had already crossed the Jordan once so now he's on the other side. He is fortunate to have the coat because without that power, there were no boats, cruise ships, or submarines to take him back to the other side. He has no choice but to use the power. The only choice you have is to use the power. Like Elisha, God will put you in positions where the only thing you can do is to go forward. He smote the water with the coat and the same waters that parted for Elijah, parted for Elisha.

Moreover in my closing of this chapter, there are probably over 50 eyewitnesses that are casting bets that you're not going to make it. People that live in the same household, people that work with you, and people that barely know you, are fervently waiting on you to fail. Those 50 students that stood afar saw him and they said, "The spirit of Elijah truly rests upon Elisha," and they came to meet him and bowed to the ground before him.

When God told me that He was getting ready to do supernatural things in my life, He warned me to be careful of the people I bring along with me. He said if they weren't around in my evening, they don't need to be there for my morning. Let me explain. If there are people that pop up when God blesses you or anoints you and they weren't there during the season of darkness in your life, they can't appreciate what God has done for you. Many people will stand around and clap and scream "Hercules, Hercules," appearing as cheerleaders when they don't even know the history of the team you're on. Sometimes you will get side tracked by people who are screaming hooray for you and you feel they love you. Don't you know every cheerleader doesn't like everyone who's on the team? For some people, cheerleading is just a way of getting attention or a publicity stunt.

These 50 men bowed down and said, "We see the spirit of Elijah on you BUT… it is possible that Elijah has fallen on some mountain." And in the next few verses they began to worry Elisha saying that Elijah wasn't dead, he's probably on a mountain and you need to go find him along with three men. You may often ask yourself the question that Elisha must have asked himself in this situation. Why are people meddling in your past? They see you have changed so why are they bringing up stories about your baby's daddy? They see you've been going to church, why are they going back before you graduated from high school? I propose this to you; they have to go back to your past because they can't relate to your current. You know you've outgrown people when all they can talk about is your past.

These 50 men continued to say that Elijah is somewhere hanging out on a mountaintop. And they strongly pressed on Elisha in that he said to them go ahead and go find him. And they sought for Elijah's body for three days and came up empty handed.

People will be searching for stuff to try to mess up the next move of God in your life. They will go out of their way to bring up false charges, accusations and allegations to block God. There are people who don't believe you can stay out of the sheets until you get married. There are people who don't believe you can stay away from drugs, alcohol, and a life of crime. When they can't find anything they say, "There's something that they're doing, I haven't figured it out yet!" But even if it was something that they thought they could put their hands on, God has already taken it and thrown it into the sea of forgetfulness.

They began to urge Elisha so much that he became ashamed. Sometimes people can embarrass you when they do things. For instance, when you take them to restaurants and they put all the Sweet'n Low in their purse or grab all the extra crackers from the

The Prophetic Coat

table at Denny's. You're not guilty are you? And so the 50 students tugged at him, and that he made him ashamed. He told them, "You saw me when I received the coat, you saw me when I used the coat to smote the waters, yet you bow down to me and declare submission." Ladies and Gentlemen, I must tell you this. People are going to see the change in your life. They will see the supernatural things God is going to do in your life. But don't let them make you go around chasing things that are gone. Elisha sat there for three days while they searched for a dead man. But guess what? He didn't die. What they were searching for was not even in the earthly realm anymore. Elijah had been transferred up to heaven. But they were looking for a body so they could have some traditional ceremony. But God says that in this next move, you won't be able to go back to traditional stuff. The 50 students came back with no evidence. I say to you that the onlookers who doubt you, are going to search for your past mistakes and come back with no evidence.

Elisha tries out his new coat (The prophetic in action)

Elisha said to them, "I told you, you wouldn't find him." Now this new prophet is in Jericho and Joshua had already cursed Jericho when he was in leadership. Elisha's first assignment with his new coat on begins in a city that is unproductive. And the men of the city said unto Elisha, the situation of this city is not pleasant. If he was looking from the natural eye, he may have said these are some real good people. But God isn't looking for "real good people." God is looking for you to catch the anointing and run with it.

The men told Elisha that while these are pleasant people, there is a situation in the city. The waters that are here are bitter and the ground is barren. Doesn't that sound like some of our churches? Doesn't that sound like some of our husbands and wives or people we work with everyday, or people you go to sweet communion with? They are in the church but there is no activation of the anointing.

Now with this anointing that God is releasing on your life, don't expect for all of your problems to go away. Don't think you're going to just tiptoe through the tulips. But like myself, I know you know that everyday won't be Sunday. But let me drop this into your spirit. Even though everyday won't be Sunday, God is placing that coat on you so that you can go through and weather the miserable Mondays and the terrible Thursdays.

I would like to share with you Elisha's first experience with his first miracle. Elisha and his team arrived in a city. The drinking waters are dirty and contaminated. Elisha requested a new bottle and he put salt into the bottle with water. He spoke a word and the waters were made whole.

Symbolically this represents that Christ Jesus is our salt and our purification. Whatever he touches will become whole. Sometimes God allows us to walk and live through some bitter situations, so he can demonstrate his power.

Elisha's training and life experiences are revealed to us, but if we wait and be trained under the proper anointing and leadership, we obtain power and will utilize these gifts that have been given to us.

It is my desire to see our students, who have the calling of God in their lives, be trained and mentored by qualified leaders. One must understand that success is not based on how smart you are. Success is based on how you finish. What Elisha has in him is now being demonstrated to the students.

I believe God will bless me to open a school of prophets training, to prepare prophets for the flock that awaits them.

I always felt different from my friends and my grandmother would always remind me that I was special and kept me in church. Because of this I was never falsely led in the wrong direction with my gift. There are many that have this gift but fall into the wrong hands of mentorship. This is where psychics and palm readers, gypsies etc.... are birthed from. So if you have a child or even you have this gift from God, protect your environment, and be aware of the company you keep, and find a man or woman of God to help you understand your gift, because knowledge is power.

I also recall my first miracle happening when I was three years old. My sister and I were left at home alone and I wandered out to get something to eat for us. I left the house to go a few blocks and on the path, I fell and deeply cut my leg on a piece of glass. I remember getting up from the ground and feeling a presence in my midst. Blood was seeping out and I remember looking at the cut and the bleeding instantly stopped. On my way back home, a neighbor saw me and she took me to her house and as she cleaned my wound, she questioned me about the cut, I couldn't explain to her what had happened. She only marveled. The neighbors took my sister and me to my grandparent's house and showed them my leg and no one could come up with a reasonable explanation of why my leg had such a severe cut but wasn't bleeding. Little did they know I had been touched by an angel. To this day I still have that scar on my leg.

It's Your Call

There are some of you that are reading this book who have a prophetic call in your life. One may ask what the gift of the prophetic is. First, God has given the calling and for no man is it self made. You are born with this gift. This gift gives you the ability to see and hear what God has revealed about people, places, events, conditions rather physical, mental or spiritual. Past, present, future, governmental, national, and international issues are also revealed by God. But the gift of prophecy is an open line of communication that is given. The Holy Spirit reveals his plans and guides us into truth. You can't get into a prayer line and receive this gift. Some people have made themselves a prophet by observing and mimicking the words that are released by the prophets of God. They then began to prophesy out of what they've heard or what they see with the naked eye. These are the ones that God warns us about. They tell lies in God's name and say things that God has not said. The 13th and 14th chapters of Ezekiel enlighten us on these false prophets.

Let me share some of my personal testimony. When I was 12 years old I began to see things before they would happen. At that time people would call them premonitions. The church that my family was attending was not yet educated on the prophetic anointing, so they as well as my grandmother labeled me as just a special child.

By the time I was 17, this gift began to happen more often. I would be with my friends and I would give them warnings about things that would happen. I just assumed they were just ideas that came to my mind. But it never dawned on me that this was a gift that I had within. And because there was a lack of knowledge, I never received mentorship or guidance concerning my God given gift so therefore my gift was left dormant for many years.

The Anointing in Motion

I discussed the experiences that I would have with my grandmother. She would share with my aunt about the Spirit of God that was in my life. I remember when I was 18 years old I was with my boyfriend and some of my friends. They had been drinking and we were going about 80 miles per hour. I told my boyfriend that there was a train around the corner and no one believed me. They laughed it off. I told them something, (which was the Holy Spirit, I just didn't know it) had told me that it was around the corner. Sure enough when got around the corner there was a parked train. He slammed on brakes and the car skidded and turned off the road and was headed directly into the parked train. The supernatural hand of God brought the car to a complete halt. Everyone except me received minor injuries and no one had to be hospitalized. These are true markings of a chosen vessel. Most prophets have near death experiences, strange encounters and unexplainable events occur in their lives.

At 23, I began to have demonic attacks. I would see demons and have these encounters which caused me to walk in fear. Yet there was no one to explain or give me any answers. My boyfriend who had then become my husband, thought I was going through these attacks because of the death of my grandmother. Then I began to have open visions which are situations where you see things while wide awake. I never got an understanding until I was 28. When I surrendered my life totally to God, my coat began to change. Then when I was baptized in the Holy Spirit, the gifts began to mature. Everything about me changed. I was in a spirit filled church and began to be mentored and given and understanding of the gift that God had given me. One night in service, my Co-Pastor laid hands on me and the gifts were fully activated. That night when I got home, I had dreams and received the gift of the interpretation of dreams. I was given the nickname of the dreamer. But I must warn you that not all dreams are from God. Some dreams come from your daily activities, conversations, personal desires and from what you watch.

There are three voices speaking in earthly realms:
- **God *(The Holy Spirit)***
- **Yourself**
- **Satan**

It is highly important that you know the voice of God. Once you know the voice of God, it will become easier for you to distinguish when He is speaking. How is this possible to decipher among the three?

1. **You must** spend time with God in prayer, more prayer, and more prayer.
2. His word. **You must** read your word and in the word you will find God, and His will for you. In knowing God you will begin to understand there are things that He does not speak because it is not in His character or will. So therefore it would either be you or Satan speaking.
3. **You must** be baptized in the Holy Spirit. This cannot be accomplished if you're not in a spirit filled church or environment or spirit filled people.
4. After being baptized in the spirit, you must walk in the spirit and be led by the Holy Spirit.

If you purchase a never-lost navigating system and never use it, then it is useless to you. How can you know where you're going if you don't turn it on? So when you're baptized in the spirit, it is there to help lead and guide you. And if you don't allow the Holy Spirit to lead you, then you, or Satan will take the lead and will have a catastrophic ending.

Now I want you take note that a lot of the experiences I shared with you was before I became a Christian. I reiterate to you that you are born with these gifts and God won't take them from you just because you're a sinner or you have sinned. The gift comes without repentance. But if you don't lead the life God has called for you to live, He will allow you to be deceived by your own emotions. That is a terrible way to live because you will always be in a world of fantasy appearing real only to you.

Remember Satan can give you a word. And if you're not careful and unable to distinguish his voice from God's, you will become a false prophet. And through disobedience and living in sin, you allow yourself to become open to demonic spirits.

Important Message: I stress the fact that you must be mentored in a spirit filled church. One must seek guidance of a leader who inhabits the prophetic gift themselves. One also needs a mentor to guide them in conserving these gifts of the spirit until they mature. If not, they will be delayed and labeled as crazy because no one around you can relate to what you are experiencing. In the old testament of the Bible, they had a prophetic school in which I've shared in this chapter.

As being a prophetess of the Lord, you will always feel different and sometimes feel left out when you don't fit in with the crowds. God will call you out from among everyone and separate you. True prophets are considered strange and they bare loneliness. Your desire is different from everyone elses. But if you obtain this gift, share it with your Pastor; seek out others who have matured in this gift, because the enemy will use the lack of knowledge to fight you because you don't understand what is taking place in your life.

The prophetic anointing is a God given gift and He gives to whomever he chooses. One day you will recognize that your time has come and you must arise to the occasion.

At the age of 30, I was ordained as a prophetess. And even now I still have mentorship in my life at my age. **But remember my dear brothers and sisters, don't despise the gift, just get an understanding so that you may do the will of the Lord that He has destined for your life. In all your getting, get understanding.**

Take that coat God has given you, that anointing shall open doors that have been closed and turn bitter waters to sweet. If you think you have missed your calling, check again. God has never misplaced anyone.

Chapter 6

The Widow's Coat

My final chapter is dedicated to widows. It is entitled the widow coat and subtitled the dark tunnel. It is dedicated to all widowers & widows that have taken the walk down the dark tunnel. This widow chapter is written from my personal experience. It is my desire and my prayer that this chapter will release healing and guidance to millions of widows. I personally feel that the loss of a spouse cannot be compared to any other loss. In wearing this coat, life can become foggy. This is when a widow is driving around (everyday) in the fog. They can't see, can't feel anything but the pain and all that is left is an empty coat, and no one can wear that coat because it doesn't fit anyone else. Besides that person is now gone.

The closet is full of coats, personal memories, and personal items. The clothing that remains in the closet still carries a scent. It's like a child who runs outdoors on a cold freezing morning to catch their school bus. As they rush to catch the bus, they leave their coat. Even though it's cold outside, the bus driver won't turn the bus around because there are other rounds to make. In comparison when you lose a loved one, it feels as if they run out the door to catch the bus. They've forgotten their coat and you run after them so they can get it. But death has rounds to make and waits for no one. So as the widow, you are left with the coat. You're left only with the evidence that someone once was there.

To open up a few pages of my heart, I will share my time wearing the widow's coat. I was only 28 years of age with three children when my husband was killed in an automobile accident. I asked the question that many of you have previously asked. "WHY ME?" For a long period of time, I walked around like a zombie going through everyday motions. Most people that are around you do not even realize that you're living your life walking in and out of a cave. Before long I was performing like a Hollywood actress. In the daytime, I was the nurturing mother and at night the grieving wife. It is good to be active. But staying busy to suppress the hurt could become dangerous. I realized that no one could live two lives and have a healthy life.

To those of you whom ask the question, "Why?" I am not sure if God answered my question back then. If He did, I am not sure if I was listening to His voice. I was not able to comprehend or understand God's Divine Will at that period of my life. My grief was buried deep within my soul. The pain as a young widow is no less than an older widow, because pain doesn't have an age limit.

As I saw the light that oozed through the tunnel and shined upon the faces of my three beautiful children, it lifted my spirits. I realized that the almighty God had entrusted me to raise them. I was the only hope for any normalcy in their lives. I realized what time does not heal, God will. I cannot imagine any widow walking through this tragedy without a personal relationship with Jesus.

I would like to pause for a moment if by chance you are reading this chapter right now and you do not know Jesus as a personal Savior, lay this book aside and repeat this simple prayer; **"Lord Jesus I am sorry, please forgive me. I have come to the knowledge that I am lost without you, and today I hereby accept you as my Lord and personal Savior."** Now let's continue the journey.

Through my experience, I have discovered that some widows knew God and loved God. After their loss they became angry with Him and made a decision not to talk to Him anymore. They have now slipped into a dark cloud of blaming Him for the loss of their loved one. Even though we do not like to be reminded, the scripture reveals God's map concerning each individual. In the book of Job, it states that every man is appointed to die. The reality is that God sets the appointment for death. It is secured and locked in His office. God in His infinite wisdom knows that we do not have the power to let go. Therefore, when your mother gives birth to you, your extension of life has already been set. I want to encourage you to let go of the grudges that you're holding against God. Pray for HIS understanding of why your loved one was taken away. It is HIS desire that you totally recover and become whole again.

I was young at the time of the loss of my husband. I had received Christ as my personal Savior three months before my husband died and therefore I am grateful. I unveil my coat today and I take you to the scene. It was a sunny beautiful Saturday in Florida; my husband had just returned home from work approximately 1:00 p.m in the afternoon. He arrived home in the company of one of his employees. He was currently a supervisor for Emergency One, a organization that builds emergency fire trucks. This is was ordinary Saturday, because most Saturdays we made it a family day. He made the decision to take his employee home and he said he would be right back. He walked over and asked me if there was anything I needed, and I responded by saying I needed to go to the beauty parlor. He gave me money and a kiss, a kiss that I did not know was to be the final one. I watched as our three year old son ran to him to go along for the ride. I watched him lock his son in the seat behind him of a 280 Z car to travel a short distance.

My two daughters and I are prepared to leave. As I recall, fifteen minutes later I heard the screeching wheels of a car coming around the corner of my home. When I looked out the door, I saw a friend of mine running and screaming. She had just witnessed my husband's car accident. I jumped in the car with her to head off to the scene that was only seven minutes from my home, only to arrive to see the victims lying in the road. However at the time, the paramedics and one doctor happen to be on that same road. (Ironically I worked with the doctor at the hospital.)

While he attended to the victims, I began to look for my husband. I discovered him lying beside the car from which the fire department cut him out of, with sheets pulled over his face. Only glimpsing at the car I could see the drivers' seat pushed to the back seat from the impact of the accident. That was when I remember that my son was locked in the seat belt behind him. At this point I was going into shock. I began screaming, "Where is my son?" At that time my husband's co-worker, who only suffered minor injuries in the accident, walked over to me and this is the beginning of the first miracle.

My husband had made a decision and rerouted to his sister's house because my son wanted to play with her son. He agreed to leave him there for a few minutes because he enjoyed his family. This was no short of a miracle and it was ordained by God that he made a short stop and dropped off our son. With a few minutes left in his last rightful decision, he saved the life of our son. I decided at that point to pull the sheets back because the doctor had already pronounced him dead. Here is the next miracle.

I pulled the sheets back and searched for a pulse. I found a faint small pulse in the artery of his neck. Because I was a heart technician, I immediately started CPR and scream for help. The highway trooper, who called for the paramedics, assisted me and that same trooper pulled me off of my husband and away from the scene. I would never forget the expression of the doctor as our eyes met. He was speechless and shocked to know that it was me. My husband was transported to the local hospital. Apparently after working on him, he died again. I was called to the back of the hospital only to be shocked by the expression that was on my husband face. I remember falling to my knees and praying. As I was praying, my husband legs began to move. He was revived and airlifted to another hospital in another city. At this point I have witnessed three miracles.

What started as hours in the emergency room turned into a long journey of three months. I must skip and by-pass scenes of this journey, at the personal request of my children. They requested no more detail be revealed and I respect their request and I am sure that you do too. They suffered loss also.

Now I begin the scene of the final road home. It is three months and I have spent everyday of those months sleeping on cots and floors of the hospital. As you can imagine, I experienced every horrible thing that could go wrong. It did in the hospital.

It was a Friday afternoon and my husband was scheduled to leave the hospital and be released into a rehab on that Monday. The attending physician came to us at 3:00 p.m. and requested to do a test, which consisted of checking fluids on his brain. I recall this scene as if it was yesterday; We were watching the Oprah Winfrey show while we waited and I was sitting beside his bed. The show consisted of different people who had experienced going through the tunnel of death. After the first testimony, my husband told me that he was going to heaven. I became very upset and refused to listen. Now I realize that he was trying to say goodbye, but I wanted to say good morning.

You must remember I was a young woman who had the wedding of her dreams. I was also a young Christian of three months. Dying was not an option for me. At this time, they began transporting my husband upstairs for the testing. I headed for the snack machine, not realizing that after three months this test would become horrific and be the final test. I returned to his room only to meet the chief surgeon. I recalled him pulling his cap off and sitting down beside me, to inform me that an accident had taken place through the hands of an intern. The intern accidentally hit an artery in my husband's brain therefore putting him in a coma. Only for a few hours he remained in a coma state. Because I had seen the power of prayer, I knelt down beside him once again to pray. I experienced for my first time a prophetic open vision. I saw my high school sweetheart. The man that I loved was in a white robe, but many people surrounded him. I remembered them being happy people singing songs of joy. I saw nothing but rows and rows of happy singing people. As I arose from my knees, I pondered in my mind what this meant. As I rose and looked into the face of my husband, I saw the sun setting. As I turned to my mother-in- law, the nurses and doctor walk over and pronounced him dead. The sun faded below the horizon.

Now that I have shared a part of my life, it is time to share the healing process. Moving forward is rarely accomplished without a considerable amount of loss grief or sorrow. Sometime moving on comes with the bitter and sweet milestone, but we must be grateful and count our blessings one by one. Some of us have been blessed; we have shared love and happiness with the one we love. Walking with them gave us knowledge, guidance, and support that shaped a part of our lives through their influence. Now that journey has come to a halt and we must move on.

While continuing this journey, your sorrow may be profound and full of rainy days. I speak as a witness and a survivor, knowing that the clouds will clear and the sun will shine again. Hope will shine a glorious light on your future and yes there will be challenges but as you continue this journey, you will be released to soar on the horizon. God will open the sky before you. Written in a heavenly glow, the sunlight will shine on your tomorrow. Selah.

I prophesy to you a new season and that a fresh breath of God will over take you in the name of Jesus. I command you to walk in the grace that will be given to you. And depending on where you are in your grieving process, you may not even want to embrace this grace, because of your sorrow. But God in his infinite wisdom and his sovereign love extends this gift to us any way. Psalms 23 states, that He maketh you to lie down in green pastures.

This chapter also offers a guideline for a road of recovery. I have a vision and passion that every widow that reads this book will be delivered and freed from loneliness. Whether you lost a spouse by way of accident, long-term sickness or disease, we share the same pain. The pain remains the same as those who lost a spouse in the New York twin towers or the Pentagon. My brothers and my sisters believe that God will heal all wounds. Life is full of journeys that consist of disappointments and sorrows. Remember that "THIS IS NOT YOUR FINAL DESTINATION."

Often times in our society, widows do not have anyone to guide them or to show them the way to recovery. Many widows live year to year suffering and wasting away and do not know when enough is enough. When I made the decision to write this chapter, the Holy Spirit gave me a release.

Because you have the coat, several changes must take place. Your spouse dies and if the Lord won't allow them to return, that means that their time has expired. Because the dead have no feelings and can't feel the cold weather, there is no need for a coat. If they are born again and die in the Lord, they have entered a place where they are covered and secured by His spirit.

Let's go to class

The Widow Coat
The Coat of the pain

My personal advice on the steps you should take:

- **Remove the coat!** They are not coming back home. There stands a gulf between you and them. That increases our pain because in our hearts we realize they are not coming back.
- **Find a friend!** In this time of your life there is no need to push everyone away. Yes, there are times when we need our space and our time alone, but for the most part, you don't need too much time alone. Surround yourself with the people who love you the most (close friends and family).
- **Get the coat out of the house!** It's not just good enough to remove it from the closet. What I'm trying to say is remove all personal belongings. Put the pictures away until you are strong enough to deal with the memories. You say how will I know? Because it won't hurt anymore. The scar will remain but there's no more pain. Jesus told Thomas to thrust his finger in his wound. Why? Because it didn't hurt anymore. The hole was just a scar, evidence that there had been a loss.

Clothing and pictures bare pain. At times some family and friends won't understand why you have put these things away. They will try to remind you of the past because they don't realize that you are trying to leave a place of hurt. Since they misunderstand you, they continue to help you carry these things around and don't realize that it's killing you softly.

Sometimes the fog is so thick that we can't see. This thick fog that blinds us represents the pain in our hearts. We are driving around with an empty coat in the passenger seat. Sometimes people who are around us don't understand. They see us, but they only see us going through the motions. They think that we have it all together and little do they know we're driving but there is a film over our eyes.

On the inside we feel abandoned and lonely. And because the fog will linger around, you need a passenger to ride in the front seat to help point the way that will lead you to the clear road. In some cases, you will even need a driver because the film over your eyes is so thick that you can't even see your hands in front of your face. But don't worry! If that is your situation, **God will send someone to hold your hand.**

Most children can sometimes bounce back quicker than adults. That is because children have a gift that God has given to them in moving on. Often times it's the very young kids who have this gift.

On a Personal Note

For many years, I couldn't heal even after I had accepted the Lord. My hurt wasn't in church, but my war was at home.

Helpful Hints:

- Have a strong prayer life.
- Stay busy (Spiritually and Socially) in all arenas.
- Become Charitable (Give of yourself to freedom). When you bless others, you free yourself.
- Travel (Go around the world).
- No graveyard visits (Including grave sites or memorials).
- No viewing of funeral videos or pictures.
- Avoid attending any funerals (3 to 5 years). Don't try to be Superman or Superwoman. Send flowers, leave messages; doing otherwise will only hinder the healing process.
- Sell your home or rent your home. If you can't do either, remodel the home. Get rid of all their personal paraphernalia, that includes the bedroom set (change the entire scene). Some people may not understand this gesture and feel that you didn't love your spouse or you've gotten over them too quickly. That is not true because you must move on. If you don't move, you will die from the inside-out. It has been predicted that most spouses die within two years of the loved one dying. But you can change the prediction.
- Sell or give away cars and personal belongings. If you have children, you may want to put these things in storage for later on in life. If you don't move in this direction, you will lose time and therefore experience unwanted sickness.

On another Personal Note: Road of Recovery

I experienced 5 years of sickness, and after 5 years, I had beat all odds. I moved my family 17 miles in the suburbs and sold my home. My healing process began. Two years later I took an even bigger move and the healing process was completed. And now I have raised my children and I'm ready to go wherever destiny leads me. In doing this, my children have healed and are able to embrace their destiny for themselves.

And finally my brethren, trust God with you. God chose the time of death for your loved one, because He's the one that is writing the story, we are the characters. He gives us the chapters and we just don't know the totality of what number He may place us on because He's the one that takes the pen and writes the end when He's ready. You don't get another chapter with that spouse.

Some widows are chosen for another coat, which includes another life. He opens the door; now walk in the path that God has chosen for you. In doing so, he will choose your next spouse, friends and social groups. This coat has to be taken off. Don't die in the tunnel. Remember that God only allowed the Children Of Israel to moan thirty days over Moses. God took the microphone and made a bold announcement and introduced Joshua as the next leader. There is nothing wrong with moving on. A widow's coat is pretty at the time of death and draws lots of attention, but after six months, it's not so pretty. To keep it on is a bad sign. Take it off and let the change begin within so that it will reflect on the outside. If God didn't want you to live and move on, He would have stopped your clock as well.

Widowhood is like a pair of traveling shoes. There will be many roads you must travel. Some will be familiar and some will be unknown. In my experiences, it is not the road of the unknown that is the hardest to travel, but it is the one that runs you down memory lane that makes you lose balance. This road reminds you of the love you and your spouse once shared; the long drives home, the small talk, the long talk, the laughs, the tears, the joy that being a family brings - rushing to take the kids to school and off to work. The stroll in the park to get the dog "Spot" out of the house. The shops, the mall, and Mr. Brown's cleaners, where you each took turns dropping of the clothes. The things that are familiar are always the hardest to let got of and move on.

My brothers and sisters, this is when you have to lean on the Holy Spirit to help you. And it is at this time that God will step in and breathe on you and cause you to forget. When He removes a spouse He knows the void that it brings, so He takes that space and time and places Himself right where it hurts. And before you know it, doesn't hurt anymore.

Then there is the unknown that is sitting there waiting for you. This road of the unknown doesn't hurt but it brings about fear. But if you can, remember that God is right there for you. Let me offer this simple example. It is like a mother and father that are standing a far off from their child and coaching them to take a baby's first step. The parents are standing on the other side smiling and clapping their hands encouraging the baby to walk towards them. But because the baby is accustomed to the support of the parents, it becomes reluctant to make that step. But when the baby looks in front of him and sees his parents so excited, they will eventually take that step of faith. The baby may stumble and began to wobble and just may fall. But because there are arms extended out, he gets up and takes a few more steps and before long, the child is walking on his own.

Your father is standing in front of you and the Holy Spirit is there to help you. He is beckoning you to take those steps towards recovery. It may be hard to start from the beginning and there will be a period of instability, but you've got to keep moving forward. "Moving forward is rarely accomplished without a considerable amount of pain and sorrow." But I announce to you that coat will change with each step you take towards your freedom!

In my final address, some widows will never marry again. This is not a sin. Some widows will find a place of fulfillment like the widow in the Bible. According to Luke 2:26 there was a widow by the name of Anna who was a prophetess who was married for seven years and her husband died. However, she remained a widow and moved into the church and gave herself completely for the use of God's kingdom. She was 84 years old when she began to prophecy to Joseph and Mary, the parents of Jesus, concerning the suffering he would endure. Anna found her purpose and also found peace. Anna was given a portion of grace that kept her from sinful relationships. No one should attempt this road with out Christ leading you. Don't fool yourself into thinking that you will never marry again. This is a trap the devil would rejoice in seeing you become entangled. Being alone isn't for everyone. It is for those such as Anna, who have been graced for that task.

There are some widows who have made marriage an art and cannot live alone. In saying this, it doesn't not make one weak, neither is it a sin in wanting to marry again. It's a matter of stepping up to the plate and confronting the issue that you were not cut out to be by yourself. In I Corinthians 7:39, the Apostle Paul wrote, "A widow is free to marry again, as long as the spouse is a born again Christian." Single life is not for everyone. Being single can be a tremendous amount of pressure for those that have not been graced for it. This is extremely dangerous when a widow does not have the power to sustain. Often times this will lead into a path of destruction and sinful relationships that will put a strain on the spirit dwelling inside. Marriage is honorable and whether you marry or remain single, your relationship with God is an independent journey. Marriage does not ensure acceptable service to God, but it's a personal commitment.

I want to encourage any widow that is considering marrying again. There will be fears of the next spouse not meeting up to the qualifications of Jane or John Doe. Guilt will also try to find an entrance because you want to move on. For example: the Florida orange. When you pick an orange, that orange will have a hull. Hulls represent the covering that a spouse brings. The seeds are the children that you produce. In order to taste the inside you must cut it in half. One side may be bitter versus the other may be very sweet. The bitter symbolizes Death. The taste of death is never sweet and is unpleasant. The sweet side represents moving on and enjoying the rest of what God has in store for you.

Take pleasure in knowing that another spouse can offer just as much fulfillment as the last one, especially when God chooses for you. I declare unto you today that God loves you and in knowing this, I hope you will find a sense of peace. God's love for you is much stronger than the sting that death leaves. The shadows of death will flee and surrender and your new horizon will break forth. Remember that the pain you've experienced will not last forever. If you allow God to pass you the next coat that He has tailored made for your journey, you will realize that the coat you are wearing, doesn't fit anymore.

Just like any other coat, the Widow Coat wasn't design to last forever. I took that same journey and I'm a Survivor!

Selah!

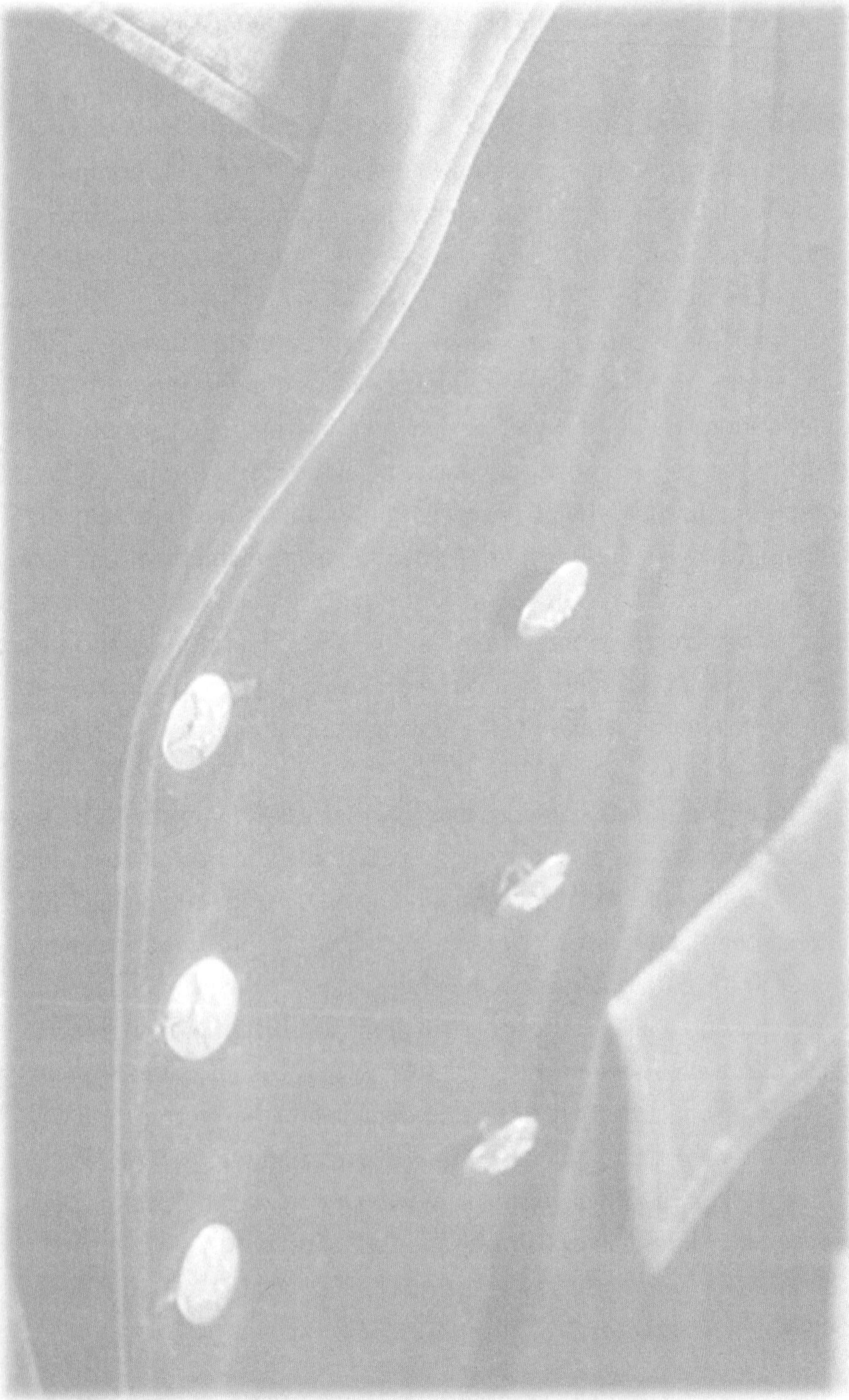

Chapter 7

A Widow's Road to Recovery

The recovery process can be a slow process. Sometimes it can be hindered by the lack of support. The best support that a widow can receive is the support of a good listener. There are moments when a widow needs to vent. There are four things that normally happen to the people that surround widows:

- They feel sorry for that person and join in their grief.
- They think you are weird or sick.
- They don't want to be a bother because they feel uncomfortable.
- There are some that don't have a clue; they want to help but feel unqualified.

Listening plays a vital role in recovery. When you don't have someone to talk to, you will find yourself talking to the deceased spouse. Even though it feels normal, in retrospect it is abnormal, because the dead cannot hear nor can they respond. It is important that when the opportunity presents itself, you must open and pour out. It's sort of similar to a sink. Once so much junk gets in, you become clogged and when you're clogged you begin to lose your function or purpose. And without an open pathway, God cannot replenish you and make you whole again.

Become a Good Listener:

Here is my advice to the people surrounding widows. When they begin to talk, let them empty out. If widows don't pour out, it will eventually lead to medical problems. At the age of 28, I began to have medical problems. I refused to listen to people and would become very upset when they tried to console me or encourage me. Because I rebuffed them, I began to suffer from anxiety attacks. Anxiety attacks occurred because I chose the route of suppression versus dealing with the loss of my husband. This went on for over two years. I went from having anxiety attacks to having heart problems. My heart valve prolapsed, and my heart rate was to be compared to that of an 80-year-old woman. Truth be told, I was suffering from "broken heart syndrome."

That's why I encouraged you to become a listener. Don't pay attention to their act that they put on when all the lights are on. But it's when all the people are gone and the lights are off that loneliness creeps in and shuts the door. And behind that door is a dark tunnel drawing them into crevices of despondency.

Broken Heart Remedy:

People that you love such as your children, grandchildren and friends will want to help with the healing process. Let them get involved. In allowing this, your broken heart will mend faster. My three children were my healing ointment. Life must move on. Get very active and avoid isolation at all cost. Isolation will bring forth thoughts that will lead into severe melancholy. Unaware, you will begin to walk on dangerous territory with isolation because you leave room for the devil to speak and find false comfort in his words.

Secondly, monitor television programs, movies, and music because the eye-gate and ear-gate can drive one to the "death-gate." Let me explain: Stay away from things that will make you reminisce. Scenes from movies that are romantic or have death involved will interfere with the healing process. They will also cause an eruption that will spiral into tormenting dreams. Take control over what you watch.

And don't be ashamed to say, "NO!" Often friends and love ones will make you susceptible to things without thinking about how it will affect you on the inside. Say, "NO" when it comes to going to funerals, weddings, couple gatherings and bridal showers. It will jar the healing process. Make an attempt to avoid these types of functions at all cost. Nevertheless, some of those things are cheerful and joyous occasions but don't try to be a superhero before your time. When we don't say, "No," we allow people to take us on a merry-go-round and guess what? They will go home and go to sleep in the comfort of their mates while you are left at home walking the floor because you can't sleep. You have to recognize your "level of pain." If it still hurts, step back from it.

But as a widow you must remember that in the absence of an answer, an assumption is always made. So your family and friends will make assumptions that you're o.k. when in actuality, you are dying a slow death.

Some widows have harder times than others. Remember moving forward is never accomplished without a considerable amount of pain. Monitor your choices. Since it will take quite a bit of time, depending on how active you are, sometimes you have to push to obtain a sense of normality.

If you can't see, then stay out the fog. Sometimes widows can't see themselves. It takes an outsider to point out the areas in which you no longer have strength. Start a prayer group or get involved with one. It may be times where it appears that prayers may not be working but remember, you are in a detoxifying stage.

Nighttime always seems worst than daytime because everything is at a standstill. But prayer will suffice the words of the enemy (the terror by night). Your prayers will have to rotate before our Heavenly Father. Meditate on the word and upon its pages. There you will find rejuvenation for your spirit.

Fasting:

Fasting is a way of letting go of your mate and washing away the residue of hurtful memories. The closer you are to God, the closer you are to healing. Prior to beginning a fast you will need to check with your physician. There are different types of fasting. A few types are listed below: Liquid Fast, which consists of water and juice and the Daniel Fast, that consist of fruits and vegetables.

You can even fast from your favorite foods, television, and the telephone. Some fasts can be a day, from 6:00am to 6:00pm (sunrise to sunset). Make sure while fasting you're accountable to someone. My children always know even now when I'm going to fast. If you have some health issues, you may have to start off your fast by doing a few hours but consult your Pastor and your doctor for instructions. If you do not have a complete understanding regarding fasting, go to your Pastor. She or he will be able to provide you with material that will help you understand the purpose for fasting.

WATCH AS WELL AS PRAY!
WARNING

Watch your associations. Who and what you align yourself with can play an essential role in your successes and defeats. Be cautious when opening up your heart. The enemy is close by listening, devising a plan. Some people speak with words comforting enough to cease the ripples in the ocean. But there will always be wolves in sheep's clothing. Since your spirit has been wounded by loss, don't allow the enemy to take advantage of your vulnerabilities: financially, sexually and emotionally. During these times you have to watch the person that is comforting you. Sometimes they have hidden agendas that could consist of scheming money from you, knowing what fragile state you may be in. For example, I went through phases of bad investments and giving through my emotions. Make sure to have someone to guide you financially. If you are going to loan money, always have a written agreement. In other words rely on an accountant.

CONFESSIONS AND DECLARATIONS:

Develop a prayer life. When you pray, confess your broken heart, your loneliness, and your pain. Whatever weighs heavily upon you, confess it to Jesus. No matter if it is anger, guilt, shame, or loneliness, CONFESS IT! These confessions may have to be done everyday. Remember Jesus experienced pain through the death of his earthly father, Joseph. Remember your GOD has suffered in all manners of flesh. Cast your burdens upon him, he cares!

Does God hear your cries and confessions? My response to you is, sure He does. Whenever you begin to feel lonely that's when God steps in and sends you grace while you are waiting and healing. Remember that His grace is sufficient for you in every weakness.

I recall my husband tried twice to discuss death while he was in the hospital but I refused. That is one of the things I regret, that I wasn't a listener. Three months had passed and he was preparing for rehabilitation; surely he isn't going to die, so I believed. When I met my husband in the senior year in High School, he had a fear of dying at the age of 30. From his childhood, he had been tormented by the same dream.

In his dream he would always dream he was falling to his death. He never celebrated his birthday, even after we married. He would always say he wouldn't live to see 30. I never gave any thought because I thought it was a bad dream that he just couldn't shake. The day of his accident he told his director at his office that he wouldn't be returning back to work. I didn't find out what he had told them until after his accident. He died October 23, a month after his 30th birthday.

Be truthful to yourself

It is imperative that you share everything with God. Most people are afraid to share their need for companionship and romance to God. Personally I tell Him absolutely everything that it is going on with me. I make every attempt to rid myself of any open doors that Satan may try to enter into.

When you are sexually active and forced to go cold turkey, your sex drive will plummet into a state of dormancy. It is normal for you to loose a desire for romance altogether. Everything pertaining to intimacy shuts down, some longer than others. Often times many people cannot grasp that concept. There are often times when you don't even have a desire for intimacy. I beg to differ with society's theory that widows marry for intimacy. Nine times out ten they will quickly marry again to fill a void of loneliness. For some, marriage was deemed as an art and had accomplished every detail of the characterization of what marriage is to be. Be careful of wolves in sheep clothing.

Each widow is different. Sometimes the spirit of lust will lurk in the shadows, observing to see when your spirit is open. At any opportune moment it will try to secure a place within you. The cold shower method is only a figure of speech. Have you ever known it to work? The truth of the matter is that you are lonely. Whenever the desire begins to creep back on you, then begin to attack it with prayer and fasting. I encourage abstinence. It's God's way, and it's the safest way. It can save your life! Because of the torn state of your spirit, it is dangerous to become involved in a sexual relationship. Once you create this new soul tie on top of being broken-hearted, you put yourself in a dangerous position. You will be even more vulnerable to a spirit of discontentment because you are seeking to fill a void that only God can fill.

Prayer Strategies

You should begin petitioning God for a closer walk with Him in all areas. Ask Him to take all memories away. When you're focused on walking closer to God, the further you walk away from the dead because the dead know nothing. They don't know you're talking to them or longing for them to come back to you. Pray this prayer everyday as long as it takes. I prayed this prayer and I am still praying it.

This is a must, if you are going to make it through holidays, birthdays, and anniversaries. God has to block the death memory. I am a living witness that this prayer works. I confessed this to God during my first month. When I started confessing this, I didn't mean it. But I kept on applying it to my daily prayer life. Surprising enough one day it was gone.

God is so awesome that he will do whatever it takes as long as it takes. Now I can face it without breaking into depression. Only God can do this. What time doesn't heal, God does. Every year will get better. Get involved and live.

Declaration

It is extremely important to recover. Talk yourself out of giving up. Become your own personal trainer. The Bible speaks of King David being so low and depressed that he had to encourage himself. Daily confess that you will live and not die. You will fulfill your born destiny. You will recover. You will rise up and take control of your life. Say that you are healed because of God's word. Confess it, believe it and receive it. He sent His word to heal you.

Rise to the Occasion!!!

Finally the closing prayer, bow your head. Father in Jesus name I present my dear sisters and brothers before you. Now take the grief and pain that is so buried within the soul. Remove the arrow from their hearts and spirit. Amen

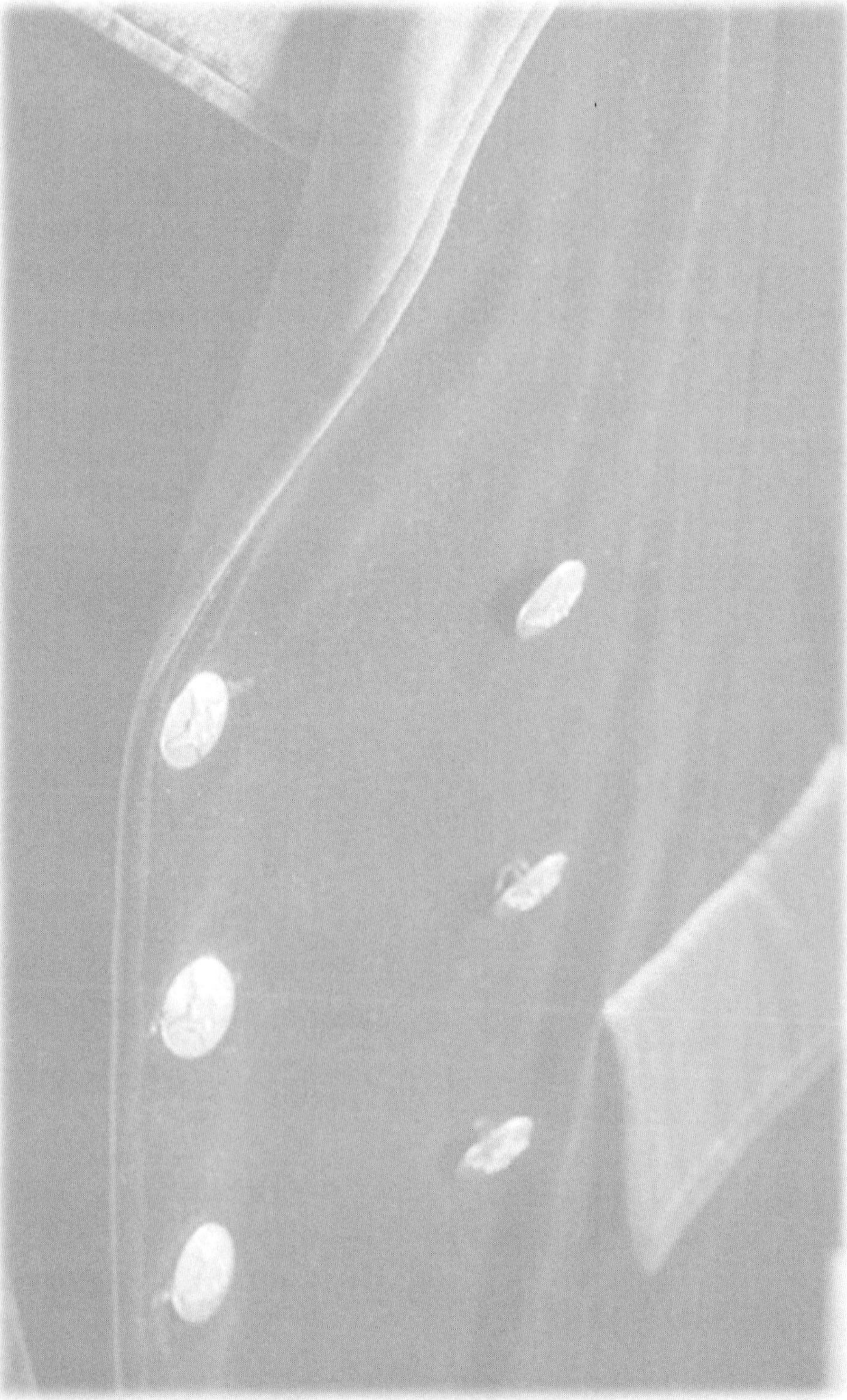

Chapter 8

The Final Tally

This book is a must read for all walks of life, because all of us have suffered delays and some of us don't even have plans to move forward. This book is written with simplicity even for the basic readers. In the writing of this book, healing is offered to the reader no matter what their ethnic background may be. This book also offers a refreshing to the body of Christ, by providing valuable insights.

This book was also written on the basis of encouraging the children of God that healing would take place. When we address the issue that we have been wearing the wrong coats for much too long. Seasons have come and gone, your sleeves on your coat are becoming shorter and yet you look in the mirror and appear to yourself as being okay even when the view from the outside reflects idiosyncrasies.

Paul said in the Romans 8 that the whole earth is in pain together and the entire world is waiting for the manifestation of the Sons and Daughters of God. Christ informs readers that all humanity is waiting for something, and some people may not know what or who that is. There is a sense of urgency that something has got to give. Christ is provoking the church to step up to plate, and be the church with a clear clarion sound.

The United States was not built on a Ethiopia Society but establishing God fearing men who were being guided by the Holy Spirit. One may say in today's society that there isn't a need for God. But I say a man left to govern himself by his own opinions and philosophies will self-destruct. A man who has no hope has no life at all. I would like to announce and introduce some words of hope and encouragement.

I have unfolded some nuggets through my writing to offer some sense of guidelines to your new future. This book is about destiny, which will ultimately lead you in a new direction. I love the scripture that says God's thoughts of you are thoughts of peace and to give you an expected end. But one must put himself in a place of expectancy and prepare to make the change. How can you move forward if the coat is too small?

"This Coat Doesn't Fit Me Anymore" is a timely and helpful book that is written from the heart and experiences I have had. It raises awareness about the delays we ignore in our daily life. It outlines profoundly the stages of widowhood, which is often overlooked in our churches. If the coat is too small, there is no room for growth. Wearing things that are too tight makes one uncomfortable and irritable. It is my prayer that by following the lives of men and women of God, you will find healing and answers to many of your questions. It is also my prayer that these answers will bless people who attend church consistently or those who rarely ever go. Remember these different coats are not for you but for God to receive the glory.

To my sisters, some of your mothers and grandmothers were trapped by the coats of abuse, because there was no escape. In times past there was no where for them to go. But you now have options that are made available to you such as shelters, rehabilitation centers, and hotlines. I challenge you today my sister to look up, walk out, and stay out. You can be sanctified, satisfied and sassy no matter what your circumstances are. You are Sarah's daughters. God said these words to Sarah; "I will bless her and she shall be the mother of nations and kings shall come out of her". Genesis 17:16

I would like to encourage my brothers that you don't have to wear the coat that your father wore; break the cycle and give your son the choice. He is the next generation; he does not have to inherit trouble. God spoke to the Apostle Peter, "Your sons and daughters shall prophesy." Acts 2:17

Finally to the widows and widowers, moving forward is rarely accomplished without a considerable amount of pain and sorrow. What time does not heal, God will! I quote to you from the Prophet Isaiah "You will not remember the reproach of your widowhood anymore, rise up and be healed and God sent His word and He healed them." Isaiah 54:4

That's why you can't hold on to them. Allow God to pass you your next coat. God has already predestined that it will help you conquer every challenge you face in different stages of your life.

Your biological clock is ticking and the timer has been set by God Himself. You cannot change your past but you can take advantage of the clock. There are three ways you make the clock work for you:

1. Make time work in your favor. Seize every moment because that opportunity may only come once.

2. Use the clock in a timely manner. Manage every hour of the day.

3. Count the days, set your goals, write them down and follow through.

Many of us have more years behind us than in front of us. Therefore we can no longer afford to make unwise decisions concerning our futures. In using these steps to take advantage of the clock, you will develop wisdom. Once you've take custody of wisdom you can accomplish your dreams, knowing how to properly execute them within proper timing of your life.

Often times we find ourselves comfortable in our current status because it doesn't cause sacrifice. You may also feel comfortable with just getting by because of the people with whom you are associated. They don't evoke you take a leap of faith, or inspire you to assimilate the potential you encompass within.

Beware of hand-me-downs. If you sort through the things that are passed down from family members, it could create generational curses, bad habits, and a continual path of failure. Failure to take inventory can result in the incessant reoccurrences of that same generational curse being passed.

May I make this synopsis? Could the reason be that our prisons are full of young people and our local jails are over crowded because those examining the coats that were being passed along in the name of "This has been in my family for years?" There are many coats that may appear fashionable to the naked eye, but as we've learned for hundreds of years following what appears to be right, can sometimes be very costly.

Each coat that God designed has a label attached, and that label will have your name on it. Each of us are **DESIGNER ORIGINALS!** Think about it. We are so unique in our Father's eyes he gave us a thumbprint barcode that will only give access to our promises by our swipe only. No two people have the same thumbprint pattern. And to think that technology just created that idea.

The reason God created and designed our individual coats is because He knew that some of our Father's would not display the character of our Heavenly Father and some of our Mother's would leave out that main ingredient of nurturing. That is why the old and the young, the rich and the less fortunate (*or should I say the procrastinators to their inheritance*), know when the time has come for change in their lives. There is always an inner perception when it's time to make adjustments. There is nothing to fear or be ashamed of. Step up to the plate with courage to refuse the Coat of Frugality. When a lack of courage is not displayed we've seen generation's succumb to a life of crime, sexual immorality, and identity crisis. The average Joe doesn't know what true love is. Love has been minimized to Hips, Lips, and Fingertips.

I would like to provoke the readers of this book to take off that Generation Coat, stand strong and bring a halt to your sons, daughters and even yourself of living a life of failure, rejection, and scarcity. Declare today that your family is free of past sins committed by your family. Proclaim to the devil that you're changing your mind set and you will no longer waste time talking about the situation and not doing anything about it. Take charge of the clock and strategize.

Apostle Paul informed us to put on the whole armor of God. In doing so we have got to put on the right coat in order to properly weather whatever storm we may currently face.

Apostle Paul put the wearing of the armor in sequential order:
- Having one spirit-lined in truth
- Having your head covered
- Having your heart covered
- Your feet protected allowing mobility.

And lastly, having our minds protected always prepared for battle. Most people spend a lifetime fighting the wrong battle because we are battling trying to prove a point to people who do not have substantial security in our destiny. In addition, we are not victorious because of doing the right thing but simply correcting the things in which we've done wrong.

Defeat is not an option. It is time for you to make steps toward change. Remember this is YOUR life story. Grasp the notion that life is full of journeys and stops along the way. In comparison to the bus system, there are certain stops they must make to let some people off and let some people on.

You must make equivalent decisions. When the season approaches, you must let some people out of your life and allow the God ordained ones in.

Embrace the changes that God offers and enjoy life. But this fullness of life cannot be embraced without the Coat of Righteousness. We must take note in the pattern that Christ laid out before us. My brothers and sisters, seek the life of Christ and learn of Him. If by chance you are asking how can you find Him, you will find Him in His word. Let me remind you he is in that little book called the "BIBLE" that you never pick up. This is the only book that has sold more copies than any other in the world. Listen, they are trying to take Christ out

The Final Tally

of everything else; don't allow the devil to take him out of your life. Once you make the decision to pick up this book, you will find guidance for your everyday living and there, you will embark a life of peace that surpasses all understanding.

In my closing, I would like to bring to your attention that Christ watched His enemies fight over His coat and while they were fighting, Christ said to Himself, they can have it because it doesn't fit anymore. You need a teacher? Jesus is the greatest teacher of all. His enemies took His coat and made Him and open spectacle. Instead of fighting He yielded to God's plan. There are many fighting, you but don't argue, do as Jesus did. Don't waste time and abort your next assignment keeping on a coat that is too small. Christ simply wore the coats that were assigned for specific seasons in His life. If you take the time to go into your prayer closet, you'll see your coats already lined up with instructions of when to put them on.

Moving on is rarely accomplished without a considerable amount of determination. Coats were never intended to be worn forever. So if this book has touched the core of your spirit, then take action and take off that coat because it doesn't fit you anymore.

The Spirit of Your Father

Genesis 3:21

After the fall of man, God reveals His sovereign love and forgiveness. Unto Adam and Eve God designed two coats and covered them with designers originals. Let your father cover you. It is His good pleasure.

Order Form

Order online: **www.sheilajministries.com**
Call Toll Free: **1-800-877-2577**
Postal Order: **S.O.L.A.C.E. International Publishing Co.
P.O. Box 680673, Orlando, Florida 32868**

Quantity	Item	Price
_____	_____	_____
_____	_____	_____
_____	_____	_____
_____	_____	_____
_____	_____	_____

Sub-Total _____
Shipping and Handling _____
Total This Order _____

(Please Print Clearly)
Name:_____
Street Address:_____
Apt.:_____ City:_____
State:_____ Zip:_____
Country:_____ Phone:_____
Email:_____
Method of Payment:
_____Check or Money Order
(Make check payable to Time of Refreshing)
_____Credit Card: ❑ VISA ❑ MasterCard ❑ American Express ❑ Discover
Card Number_____-_____-_____-_____ Expiration Date: _____/_____
Card Holder (please print):_____
Signature:_____
  (Credit card orders cannot be processed without signature)

For current shipping and handling information, call 1-800-877-2577
Or visit our website at www.sheilajministries.com